CW00418526

The Dam, a 1910 Painting based on an earlier drawing

Scenes from Sutton's Past

Edited by ROGER LEA

For The Sutton Coldfield Local History Research Group

A closer look at aspects of the History of Sutton Coldfield

Westwood Press Publications

44 BOLDMERE ROAD, SUTTON COLDFIELD
WEST MIDLANDS B73 5TD

TELEPHONE: 0121-354 5913

View of Sutton across Meadow Platt,
sketched by Miss Bracken in 1838

All rights reserved
ISBN 0 948025 10 7

© Copyright Westwood Press
First Edition Autumn 1989
Reprinted Summer 1995

Printed by The Westwood Press, 44 Boldmere Road
Sutton Coldfield. Produced by offset litho.

Contents

View of Sutton in 1840 from the Birmingham Road, by Miss Bracken, who always signed her pictures with a frond of bracken. This picture was painted in about 1860, based on her memory and earlier sketches; it shows the Olde Pie Shoppe referred to on Page 143.

Introduction

MUCH OF THE INFORMATION in this book is new, in the sense that it is not to be found in the published histories. The fruits of 8 years of research into source material is represented here, in the form of a series of articles on aspects of Sutton history by members of the Research Group. For us, studying the original sources has brought our local history to life with a vividness lacking in the available histories, and we hope something of this will be passed on to the reader.

The articles are not in date order, but are presented as a series of views of particular aspects of Sutton's history; although the contributors have a different approach to the interpretation of the material on their subject, each article is soundly based on primary source material. The first item is concerned with one particular document, compiled to satisfy the Bishop of Lichfield's Court as to the value of the moveable possessions of a deceased person, so that the will could be proved; it is one of many such probate inventories now preserved in the Diocesan Record Office at Lichfield. Some of the background evidence used in this article, however, is derived from sources at the County Record Office at Warwick — lists of all the house-holders which were compiled in order to collect the Hearth Tax just after the Restoration, and the Parish Register of all the baptisms, marriages and burials recorded in Sutton.

Many of the sources used in the next item have been published, and include the Domesday Book, Royal Charters granting markets and fairs, and the accounts of the bailiff who collected all the income for the lord of the manor. Records of the conveyance of land and property are the main source, however, from the major exchange of manors between the King and the Earl of Warwick in 1126 to the humble sale of 3 acres of land in Hill Village in 1660. Many of these property deeds are in Latin, written on parchment in handwriting which requires long study to decipher, and of obscure meaning when they refer to place names or landmarks which no longer exist. The originals were found in record offices at Stafford, Nottingham, and Birmingham, and some are still held by local solicitors.

Reference was also made to maps of a later date, and, not least, to the features still surviving in the topography of Sutton Coldfield.

Observation of the surviving features is the basis of our President, Norman Evans', piece on Sutton Park, but he has also used personal recollections, the records of a golf club, newspaper reports, and the minutes of the Sutton Corporation (known, until 1886, as the Warden and Society). This article required much painstaking work poring over maps to understand exactly what was going on where, his own maps neatly summarising his results—the sources used include Ordnance Survey maps, mainly the large-scale 6'' to the mile and 25'' to the mile series made 100 years ago; plans produced to accompany conveyances of land; and the detailed nineteenth century maps of Sutton showing every house and every field. These were produced in connection with the conversion of tithes (the Rector was entitled to one tenth of the agricultural produce) to money payments in 1824; the Enclosure of the Commons (common land was divided up and allotted to people who formerly had grazing rights) in 1850; and the division of the parish in 1856 (when the ecclesiastical parishes of Walmley, Boldmere, and Hill (Mere Green) were formed).

The history of the parish church was compiled from a variety of printed sources, but use was also made of the unpublished recollections known as the Holbeche Diary, written about 100 years ago. The fabric of the building itself was a major source of information, and physical evidence is the only source for prehistoric Sutton, summarised in Mike Hodder's article. He used maps mainly as tools to assist his research, but needed to refer in passing to the Geological Survey reports and maps for the area. Even the site of Langley Mill has gone, but the pools remain as evidence, and such diverse sources as a Corporation grant from the Borough Records in Birmingham Reference Library, a letter quoted in Riland Bedford's *300 years of a family living,* as well as wills, surveys and directories helped Ken Williams to throw some light on this elusive subject.

The next two items derive from a close study of two sources already mentioned — wills and inventories, and the parish register - and show how such sources can be made to reveal information on unexpected aspects of the life of the town. With the increasing number of written sources surviving from beginning of the 19th century, research means sifting through a mass of material rather than seizing on every scrap, and the article on the origin of the elementary schools is distilled from many sources, including the records of the Court of Chancery, evidence given to official enquiries, and the reports of the Charity Commissioners of 1833. The minutes of the Corporation were a major source, however, as were the minutes of the Fire Brigade Committee for David Chubb's article. A different class of Borough Record, the deposited building plans, was used (in conjunction with the sales catalogues of estate agents, and maps and plans) for the housing article; both this one and the Fire Brigade also involved careful study of contemporary directories and newspapers. These are held in Sutton Local History Library on microfilm, as are the enumerators' books used in the compilation of the national population censuses of 1841, 1851, 1861, 1871, and 1881 to which Janet Lillywhite referred; other sources included reports of the Medical Officer, rate books showing the owners and rateable value of every house, railway records, and, not least, the houses themselves.

It was possibly the demolition of buildings which, for many people, expressed the character of Sutton Coldfield — the Parade shops — which drove Marian Frankling to search directories and newspapers for information about the Parade's origins, and plunder the memories of those who lived there. But a major source was pictorial — she drew on the collections of photographs held at Sutton library and in private hands, and also a considerable number of paintings and drawings — sources which are not available for the local history of earlier periods, when our historical imagination has to supply pictures for the mind's eye.

For the interpretation of these sources, and the context in which they are used, each individual writer is responsible. However, it is hoped that the account of life in the 1680's will lead the reader to look back in time to the medieval period, when the park was established and the Church built, and these visible monuments of the past will arouse curiosity as to still earlier periods. The mill article brings us back to the 1680's for a closer look at life then, after which the transformation wrought in the nineteenth century is illustrated by the detailed study of a few important aspects of the life of the town.

PICTURE CREDITS:
Birmingham Public Libraries (Sutton Coldfield Local History Library) Page 2,4,6,10,12,14,23,34,36,40,49,50,52,54,56,60,61,62,64,65,71,76,78,86,98,102, 106,108,114,126,128,130,131,134,136,138,139,140,142,144,145,146,148,149,151, 152,153,154,;(Archives Collection) 28; Drawings by Stephen Lea after Lindsay, J.S. Iron and brass implements of the English House 1927, Page 15,16,86,88,92, 93,95; Staffordshire County Archivist (Lichfield Joint Record Office) Page 17, 18 (B/C/11 28 April 1685), 90 (B/C/11 1 May 1704); Norman G. Evans Page 58-59; Roger Lea 69,80,105,119; other illustrations are by the author of the article concerned.

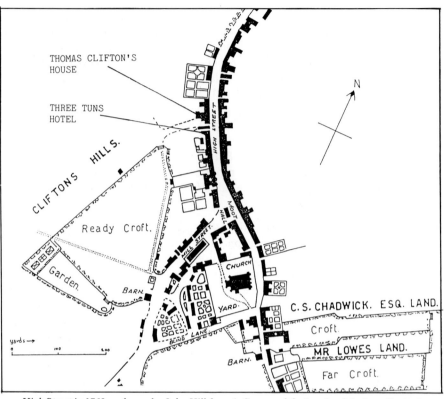

High Street in 1765, redrawn by John Hill from 'a Survey of the Lands of Andrew Hacket' made by John Snape in 1765, and now in the County Record Office at Warwick. The town of Sutton comprised less than 100 houses at the time, and Clifton's house was near the end of the town. Until 1982 there was a lane between Clifton's house and the Three Tuns known as Clifton Street. The site is now occupied by offices.

The Sutton Coldfield Local History Research Group receives support from the Workers Educational Association, The University of Birmingham School of Continuing Studies, and Birmingham Public Libraries. Members meet on Wednesday evenings at Sutton Coldfield Local History Library to pursue their research projects, and some of the completed projects are published in this book. The group has a number of other activities such as field meetings and public lectures—details are available from the Secretary, c/o Sutton Coldfield Library, Lower Parade, Sutton Coldfield, B72 1XX. Tel. 021-354 2274.

Thomas Clifton of Sutton Coldfield, died 1684

by Jim May

PROBATE INVENTORIES are increasingly recognised as valuable sources of social history, especially in the 16th and 17th centuries. The Sutton Coldfield Local History Research Group has been studying inventories, many of which are preserved in the archives of the former Consistory Court (Bishop's Court) at Lichfield. One of the more interesting of these documents is that relating to Thomas Clifton, who died in 1684.

In his will, he is described as a 'Diar and Sharman', that is, dyer and shearman; he was a skilled craftsman, who finished the rough woollen cloth turned out by the local weavers, and understood dyes and the various processes of dyeing, as well as the delicate operation of trimming the surface of the cloth with a large pair of shears. Further evidence in the will indicates that he lived in the centre of Sutton (probably in the High Street), and that his property included a house, three fields, a barn and a cow-house.

This in itself does not throw much light on how a tradesman lived in 17th century Sutton. Fortunately, the two appraisers who were appointed to take the inventory of Clifton's property were competent and conscientious men, probably neighbours, named Richard Rogerson and Thomas Freeman. They worked through the house methodically, room by room, listing and valuing every item, with no obvious omissions.

The rooms named are: on the ground floor, Kitchen; Buttery; Shop; Workhouse; upstairs, three chambers and a cockloft. Thus there were eight rooms in all, four of them available for day-to-day living, which seems a reasonable standard of housing. Nevertheless, when all the family were at home, the rooms must have been rather crowded, since they had to accommodate Thomas himself, his wife, three sons, and three daughters. On the whole, the impression created is that of an adequate, even comfortable, but far from luxurious home. How far is this borne out by the rest of the inventory, when examined in detail?

High Street in 1870, showing the site of Thomas Clifton's house
occupied by the three-storey building beyond the Three Tuns

The chambers, which correspond, very roughly, to the modern bedroom, are three in number. Listed first is the Chamber over the Kitchen. It contained one bed — a feather bed, better than those elsewhere. No doubt father and mother enjoyed this comparative luxury, as well as the warmth from the kitchen below. However, the room served more than one purpose: it also contained a table, six stools, three chairs, and a livery cupboard, besides coffers and boxes; clearly this was where the family would eat. There was a tablecloth, too, and a dozen napkins, while touches of luxury were added by the two cushions (one of silk), the two Kidderminster carpets (valued at two shillings) and the looking-glass. The carpets would be used to cover table or bed rather than on the floor, and the looking-glass was of fairly recent introduction at this level of society, not found in the majority of Sutton inventories of this date.

The overall impression is that of a sizeable room where the family could gather for meals, and sit chatting. The contents were valued at £5-12-0, the two most costly items being the bed, at £2-10-0, and the table — and bed-linen, at £1-11-0.

The next room, the Chamber over the Entry, seems to have served only as a bedroom. It contained two beds that must have been considered second best and third best, as they were valued at £1-10-0 and £1-0-0, and each is described in the same way: 'Bedstids, bed, bolster, curtaines, blankits. ' They must have been adequate but hardly luxurious; the curtains were a necessity in the unheated and no doubt draughty room. The other furniture was one chair, a stool, a press, and a coffer. Perhaps the last two items were used to hold what the appraisers call 'his weareing Aparrill and moneys in his purse' , which they valued at £3.

The Chamber over the Shop seems to have been what estate agents now call a 'utility room'. Besides the 'one bedstid, bed and beding all old ones' (valued at only 6/8d), there was a stock of 13 sheets, 6 napkins, and 3 tablecloths, all made of a coarse flaxen material called 'hurden', (sixty years ago, 'harden' aprons were still being used, in Yorkshire, for rough housework). The most valuable item in this room is entered as 'Yarne both linen and woollen, and wooll'; worth £2-8-0, it must have made a large mound, and helps to explain the three spinning wheels. These, along with the three cheese-vats, show that spinning and cheese-making were among the domestic occupations carried on, perhaps in this very room.

On the ground floor, the Buttery seems to have been where most of the other household work was done: the first entry is '3 barrills one Ferkin one Churn and one Loome', valued at ten shillings altogether. This indicates that a fair amount of brewing went on; the loome was a large open vessel or vat (sometimes called a brewing loom); the firkin would hold nine gallons of beer, and the barrels an unspecified amount. The churn would make butter from the milk supplied by the three cows (listed later in the inventory), and the brass skimmer, which was kept in the kitchen, would also play its part.

After the buttery, the appraisers moved on to the Shopp, i.e. the workshop. Here Thomas Clifton had earned his living and kept the tools of his trade: '4 pare of Sheares for shereing cloath, 3 cotting bords, 1 sheare bord, some handles', as well as 20 yards of 'woollen new cloth'. The Work-house was where he practised the other side of his craft, dyeing. It contained 'two furnies one press and pressing papers' valued at £5 (the same amount as his 25 sheep). It seems likely that the furnies were large containers in which cloth was boiled in the dye-stuff. When it was ready, it would be taken to the 'backside' or back yard, and there stretched on the 'tenters' (tenterhooks); the inventory values the 'tenters in the backside' at ten shillings.

Thus Thomas Clifton's main income would appear to be derived from work carried on in two rooms, with equipment worth £7, together with 20

Joint stools, of the type included in Clifton's inventory. These examples, possibly made locally in the 17th century, are in the Parish Church

yards of new cloth at £2. We have no means of telling if he was kept busy in his 'shop', but no doubt his equipment was adequate for a small-scale enterprise. However, as the last part of the inventory shows, he had other resources. But before considering this, let us turn to the room that first occupied the appraisers' attention.

This was the kitchen, where they listed no fewer than 50 separate items. They followed the normal routine by starting at the focal point: the hearth. Their first item is the grate, incidentally the only one in the house, and probably burning wood, although coal was coming into use in some Sutton houses. There they noted the pot-hangers, the spit, and a 'tosting iron', but there is no mention of a frying-pan or baking oven — was the Clifton diet a monotonous one of boiled or roast? In addition there were the usual adjuncts of fire-shovel and tongs, and 'cobbards'. There is some uncertainty as to the meaning of 'cobbards'; sometimes it is used as a synonym of the andirons on which the fire rested, but in its present context — 'one Spitt with Cobbards' — it must indicate another meaning, iron bars, with a knob at the end, to support a spit. Also associated with the hearth were a dripping-pan, a smoothing iron with two heaters, and a pair of bellows (valued at 3 shillings the lot). The dripping pan was put under the spit to catch the hot fat from the roasting meat, and the smoothing iron would be a box-iron into which the heaters (blocks of iron) were inserted after heating in the fire.

The other cooking utensils were three brass pots and '6 kettells brass old ones all', valued at 20 and 15 shillings respectively. The rest of the brassware included the very useful pestle and mortar, also one warming pan, a platter, a candlestick, a ladle, and a skimmer. After valuing the brass, the appraisers went on to consider the pewter: 37 items in all, to a total value of £1-6-0. Most of it functioned as what we today think of as crockery. There were 19 pewter dishes, seven porringers, a basin, and a chamber-pot; for

Fire-grate and tongs of the period

drinking, the Cliftons had a flaggon, two cans, and a cup; for other uses, two candlesticks, two salts, and a 'gaun', which was either a gallon measure or a lading-can. This quantity of pewter seems barely adequate for a family of eight, but by 1684 one of the daughters was married, and one or more of the sons had his own home, and perhaps some of the family pewter had been passed on to them.

It seems that the kitchen was used for other purposes than cooking; this is made clear by the presence of a table, a form, and '4 old cheares', as well as a dresser, two cupboards, a screen, and two shelves; there was also a bacon-rack. The last items here to engage the appraisers' attention are unusual, and interesting in that they provide a clue to Clifton's status; they are 'one parcell of Bookes one desk one looking glass and 6 quishions'. Cushions were less a luxury than a necessity on the wooden seats of chairs and forms, but the parcel (i.e. a fair number) of books and the desk, together with the fact that Clifton signed his will in a legible hand, distinguish him as an educated man at a time when many of his neighbours were illiterate.

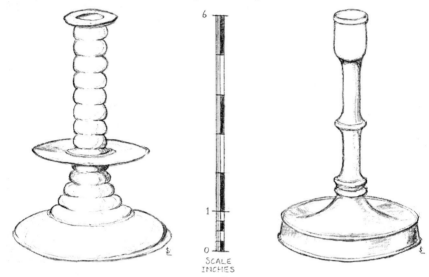

Brass candlesticks

For the final section of the inventory, the appraisers moved outdoors, to deal with another aspect, Thomas Clifton the farmer. Like many other tradesmen in 17th century Sutton, he was also a smallholder, with land behind the house and elsewhere, and the usual collection of 'live and dead stock'. Its value was just over £33, one pound more than all the rest of his goods and chattels — an indication of its vital importance to the Clifton economy.

The livestock was the most valuable, comprising 2 mares at £4, 3 cows and a heifer at £9, 25 sheep at four shillings each, and a 'sowe and piggs'. There is no mention of saddles or bridles, so it seems likely that the mares worked on the land. Corn and hay in the barn, and threshed corn, were worth £10, and 'a parcell of Muck' one pound. Other items outside, or in the barn, included 'coales and cheese and lime', and the essential cart, plough and other husbandry implements.

This completes the picture as far as we can see it or deduce it from the inventory. We have a picture of a citizen, or rather a villager, who was of middling status, not rich, but making a living. The total value of the inventory, £65, suggests that he was more prosperous than some of his

Facsimile of the last part of Clifton's inventory

Goods in the Buttery

	£ - s - d
3 barrels one Ferkin one Churn and one Loome	0 - 10 - 0
3 bords one weele one bole one sope kimnill all old ones	0 - 2 - 6
2 dressers, 2 coffers, all 10s. 6d	0 - 10 - 6
goods in the shopp	
20 yds of woollen new cloath at 40s. all	2 - 0 - 0
4 pare of sheeres for sherring cloath 3 cotting bords	
1 sheare board some handles atll 30s.	1 - 10 - 0
goods in the workhouse	
2 Furnies one press and pressing papers 5li	5 - 0 - 0
the tenters in the backside 10s	0 - 10 - 0
Corne threshed and a table 3li	3 - 0 - 0
Corne and hay in the Barne	7 - 0 - 0
2 mares 4li. 3 cowes and A heffer 9li	13 - 0 - 0
Cart plou and other Husbandry Implements	3 - 0 - 0
25 sheep 5li	5 - 0 - 0
Cow and piggs Coales and cheese and lime	1 - 6 - 8
For a parcell of odd lumber in the Cocklofte	0 - 3 - 4
A parcell of Muck 20s	1 - 0 - 0
	43 - 13 - 0
the total somme is. . .	65 - 17 - 2

17

fellow-tradesmen, like Edward Dickman, miller (£18); J. Burton, shoemaker (£36), or J Phillips, tailor (£8), but others were his equals, like his neighbour Robert Rogerson, an innholder whose inventory totalled £54. Thomas Clifton seems to have been careful with his money, for the inventory—unlike those of a good many of his contemporaries—has no mention of debtors or creditors.

All in all, you would think, a decent, sober, hard-working man, busy with his farming, his dyeing and shearing (where his son Francis, to whom he bequeathed 'all my implements belonging to my trade', no doubt assisted), while the womenfolk got on with the milking, churning, cheese-making and spinning, as well as the household tasks.

Before leaving the inventory, it seems fitting to say a word or two about the men who made it. Richard Rogerson was a mercer, and as his name appears next to Clifton's on the tax returns, probably lived next door. He seems to have been looked on as a sound and reliable man, having already acted as an appraiser for at least 6 other inventories, whereas his fellow appraiser, Thomas Freeman, was probably a beginner. His name hardly appears in the records, but later in 1685 he was one or the appraisers of the inventory of Charles Field. Their work is much more conscientious than that found in many of the other inventories for Sutton men of the time, where such frustrating entries as 'for all in that room', or 'All the pewter' are commonly found; the Clifton family were no doubt pleased with it. At all events, the appraisers themselves were quite satisfied: instead of merely signing at the bottom, they indulged themselves with a flourish:

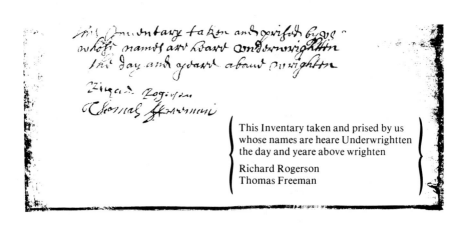

This Inventory taken and prised by us whose names are heare Underwrightten the day and yeare above wrighten

Richard Rogerson
Thomas Freeman

The Medieval Landscape of Sutton Coldfield

by Roger Lea

ARCHAEOLOGICAL OR DOCUMENTARY EVIDENCE BEING ABSENT, it would have been possible until recently to gain an impression of Sutton 1,000 years ago as primeval forest undisturbed by the hand of man. Such a view can hardly be sustained in the light of modern methods of archaeological investigation, which have shown that there was no 'significant increase in arable cultivation at the expense of either woodland or pasture between the fifth century and the eleventh'[1]; if this generalisation is true for Sutton, then there must have been a considerable settlement here before the year 500 A.D. However, archaeology in Sutton has not been very fruitful on this point, so any attempt to describe the appearance of Sutton between the 11th and 15th centuries must rely heavily on sources which have already been studied exhaustively, and be subject to correction and dispute.

The Domesday Book[2], compiled in 1086, is a survey of the assets of over 13,000 places in England, and a major source for the historian. The Sutton Coldfield entry is of considerable interest, indicating a sizable settlement or series of settlements with about 25% of the land under cultivation, 25% wooded, and 50% uncultivated heath, pasture, marsh and scrub; an indication of the probable distribution of these is given by the map.

Most, if not all, the cultivated land was organised into open field systems pertaining to hamlets or townships. At the village of Hill, for example, the village was laid out regularly along the road to Lichfield (now Hill Village Road), each house having a croft of land attached, with the three open fields beyond. There was probably some meadow ground near Mere Green. Each villager would be the tenant of strips of land in each field, and the owner or (more likely) part owner of a plough and a team of oxen to draw it. (Although Hill is not specifically mentioned in the Domesday survey, land there was granted to Canwell Priory by 1153[3], so it was probably included under Sutton). Joint ownership of ploughs and co-operative cultivation of the fields in rotation were good reasons for the villagers to live close to each other in nucleated settlements such as Hill, and the other

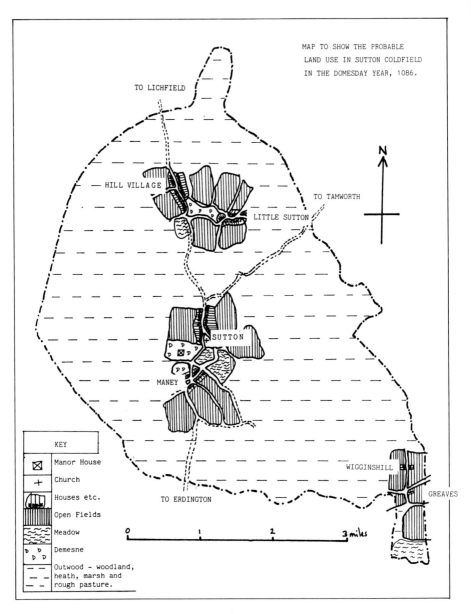

MAP TO SHOW THE PROBABLE
LAND USE IN SUTTON COLDFIELD
IN THE DOMESDAY YEAR, 1086.

TO LICHFIELD

HILL VILLAGE

TO TAMWORTH

LITTLE SUTTON

N

SUTTON

MANEY

WIGGINSHILL

GREAVES

TO ERDINGTON

KEY

⊠   Manor House

✛   Church

    Houses etc.

    Open Fields

    Meadow

ᴅ ᴅ   Demesne
ᴅ ᴅ

    Outwood - woodland,
    heath, marsh and
    rough pasture.

0   1   2   3 miles

*Schematic plan of pre-conquest land-use, based on evidence of 19th-century
field names and patterns, property deeds from the 14th-19th centuries,
present-day landscape features, and Domesday Book*

20

Sutton villages—Little Sutton, Maney, Great Sutton, and the tiny hamlets of Wigginshill and Minworth Greaves — were of this pattern. Even at this early date there is some evidence of less substantial tenants occupying small holdings on the fringes of the open fields, ekeing out their meagre crops by day-labouring and out-work.

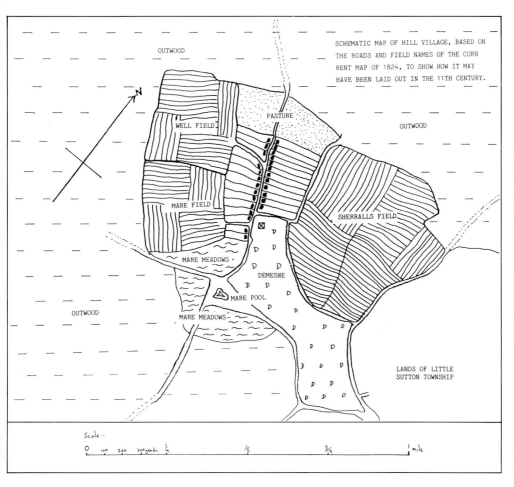

SCHEMATIC MAP OF HILL VILLAGE, BASED ON THE ROADS AND FIELD NAMES OF THE CORN RENT MAP OF 1824, TO SHOW HOW IT MAY HAVE BEEN LAID OUT IN THE 11TH CENTURY.

Plan showing Hill as a typical linear nucleated village, with three open fields and demesne — a purely schematic reconstruction

Woodland was of two kinds, depending on whether it was managed primarily for timber and wood products, in which case it would be enclosed to keep animals out, or whether it was open to grazing animals. Wood was a

21

major resource, not only for building, fencing, toolmaking etc., but also for fuel and charcoal, and the management of woodland to produce wood suitable for the various uses was well understood in early times[4]. In 1126 Sutton transferred into the hands of the Earl of Warwick by a deed[5] which mentions an enclosed wood and an outwood common to the freeholders, suggesting that both kinds of woodland were present; a deed of 1207[6] refers to property at Bulls Lane being in Sutton Woods, and the area of Sutton east of Springfield Road long bore the name 'Beyond the Woods', so the bulk of the woodland may well have extended from Eachelhurst and Bulls Lane on the east side of Sutton to Hill Wood in the north.

The remaining areas of uncultivated land consisted of heathland to the west of Sutton ('The Coldfield' extended from Boldmere to Barr Beacon) on the poorer soils there, and other patches of heath or marsh where cultivation was difficult. These areas were probably similar in appearance to the unwooded parts of Sutton Park, in which sheep and goats have likewise never been allowed to graze, and where the numbers of cattle are sufficient to prevent the re-establishment of woodland, but not so great as to result in over-grazing. Some time in the 11th or 12th centuries Sutton Chase was detached from the Forest of Cannock, but forest conditions still applied, and one of these was a restriction on the depasturing of sheep and goats, which were thought to be incompatible with the fallow deer. Fallow deer, their pursuit and their venison, were of great significance to the Norman nobility, and their conservation in forest areas tended to be of prime importance. However, living in a forest area did not prevent the inhabitants of Sutton in the 10th century from having the requisites for subsistence agriculture: 'there had to be arable land to produce crops, meadow to provide hay, and somewhere for the animals to be pastured. Woodland was a highly desirable extra, and the standard of living of peasants in the forest areas was always higher than that of their contemporaries whose villages lay in open country'.[7]

King Henry I exchanged Sutton in 1126 for a manor of the earl of Warwick, by a charter which states 'Earl Roger . . . may have one park and one hay fenced . . . an outwood common to the freeholders . . . in demesne two carucates of land and one water mill . . . and eighteen fallow deer'. The mill with its dam and pool was on the east side of Lower Parade; Lower Parade formed the dam (the line of The Parade was set out in 1826), and the pool which provided the head of water to drive the mill occupied most of the Gracechurch Centre site. Earl Roger's deer park probably made more impact on the landscape — it consisted of an area of land with woods and clearings, and at least one stretch of water, within a boundary formed by a deep ditch and a high bank topped by a fence, possibly considerably smaller

22

Fallow deer — this 19th century illustration emphasises its value as a meat animal.
(from The Royal natural history, 1894)

than the present Sutton Park; the earthworks represented a considerable achievement by the men of Sutton. There is some question as to the size of the original park, but the enclosure which can be traced on the ground today[8] probably dates from the 11th or 12th century; it passes through areas later enclosed for woodland, suggesting that at the earlier date they were open land. The creation of the deer park suggests the existence of pools, and there may have been a pool at this time on the site of the present one in Clifton Road; Keeper's Pool may also be this early. Although these pools were not made to drive mills, they had an economic value — the highly prized carp or 'meat fish' which flourished in them. Mention of these features in the 1126 deed can be read as confirming that they were already in existence then, in which case the mill could have dated from the late Saxon period, while the park was a Norman invention.

The ownership of Sutton Chase gave the Earls of Warwick the opportunity to reward their friends and allies at small cost to themselves by granting lands or privileges within the chase. Substantial grants of estates in Sutton had been made by the middle of the 13th century, at Langley, New Hall, and Peddimore, whose owners built themselves moated mansions, culti-

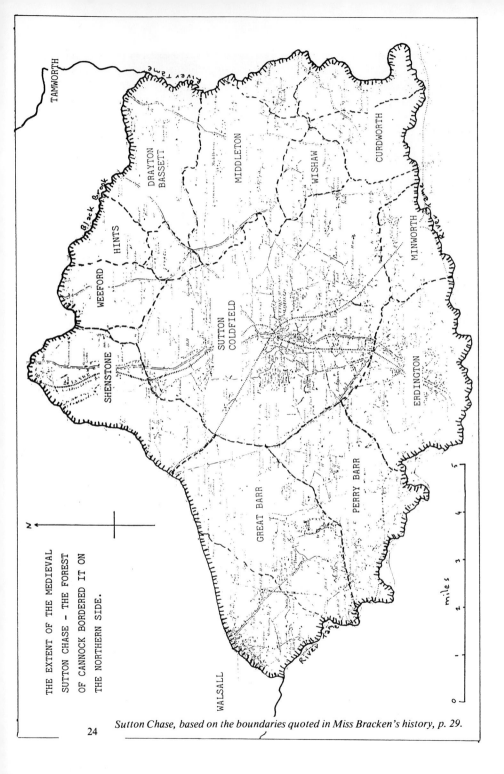

THE EXTENT OF THE MEDIEVAL
SUTTON CHASE – THE FOREST
OF CANNOCK BORDERED IT ON
THE NORTHERN SIDE.

TAMWORTH

DRAYTON BASSETT

MIDDLETON

WISHAW

CURDWORTH

RIVER TAME

Black Brook

HINTS

WEEFORD

MINWORTH

SUTTON COLDFIELD

SHENSTONE

ERDINGTON

GREAT BARR

PERRY BARR

WALSALL

miles

0 1 2 3 4 5

Sutton Chase, based on the boundaries quoted in Miss Bracken's history, p. 29.

24

vated the surrounding land, and increased the prosperity of the town. Their activities were a sign of the changing economic climate: as the population and wealth of the country increased, so suitable sites for country estates were more in demand, and the price of corn justified the cultivation of land which had previously been considered unprofitable. A large proportion of the land in Sutton was of this marginal nature, and the 13th century saw great inroads made into it. The deed of 1207 already mentioned gave permission to cultivate land at Ramshurst in Bulls Lane, and the taking in of land, or assarting, converted a huge area of eastern Sutton to farmland by the end of the century. Dugdale[9] quotes a deed of 1287 in which William Beauchamp, Earl of Warwick, granted to Thomas de Arden of Peddimore permission to fish in the Ebrook, to agist hogs in the woods of Peddimore and beat down acorns for them, to gather nuts, to take wood for fuel and hedges, and timber for buildings, to assart up to 20 acres and enclose them so that does with their fawns might leap over the hedges, and grow corn so long as the cattle of anyone having rights of common could graze the land after harvest, and to retain an assart of 4½ acres already made. This process of assarting had probably reached its peak by 1320, when the amount of land under cultivation would have been at its highest level, possibly encroaching onto the inhospitable Coldfield by the temporary allocation of allotments or 'lot acres' for short courses of tillage as was still done in the 18th century[10].

The more intensively exploited landscape of 1320 supported a larger population, — possibly over 1,000 — and Sutton had a weekly market, an annual fair, and a parish church. Being a centre for the neighbouring settlements, communication by road became more frequent, and the basic network of roads was in existence by this time; many of the roads had always served to divide the open fields, provide the village street, give access to pasture for herds of animals, but only occasionally for inter-village travel. Some of the roads consisted of a wide space between the hedges of fields or the garden plots of houses, and beyond the cultivated land the traveller could make his own way over the commons.

In 1309 a commission enquired into the customs of the manor[11], and found that the inhabitants could depasture their cattle freely in any outwoods or other common places, and anywhere from September 29th to February 2nd (Michaelmas to Candlemas) except in the Park; however, the laws of the Chase still militated against the depasturing of sheep on the commons until Bishop Vesey disforested Sutton in the 1520s. With the more intensive use of the outwood which had formerly been available for grazing, the commons of 1320 probably occupied about the same acreage as those of 1820; although the sources quoted above appear to preserve rights of

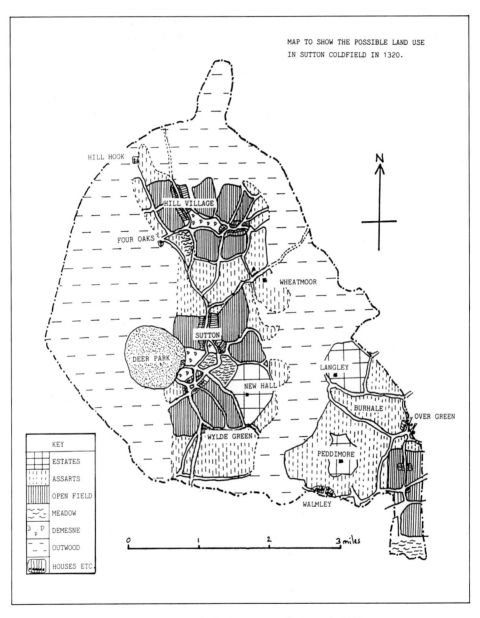

MAP TO SHOW THE POSSIBLE LAND USE
IN SUTTON COLDFIELD IN 1320.

HILL HOOK

HILL VILLAGE

FOUR OAKS

WHEATMOOR

SUTTON

DEER PARK

LANGLEY

NEW HALL

BURHALE

OVER GREEN

WYLDE GREEN

PEDDIMORE

WALMLEY

KEY

ESTATES
ASSARTS
OPEN FIELD
MEADOW
DEMESNE
OUTWOOD
HOUSES ETC.

0   1   2   3 miles

N

Schematic plan of the land-use pattern in Sutton in 1320

common in all the assarted lands, it must have been very inconvenient to have the neighbours' cattle wandering over one's land, and remedies were sought. The Parson of Wishaw issued a quitclaim in 1240 to the Earl of Warwick 'for all the assarts he has made in Sutton, reserving to myself common of pasture in those assarts', but such an agreement was probably made in order to secure satisfactory compensation when he ultimately settled with the assarters to give up his rights[12]; many other such agreements must have been made. This would have put more pressure on the remaining common, not only in respect of more intensive grazing, but also on the woodlands; whereas at an earlier time the outwoods yielded ample woodland products for everyone's needs, conservation measures, such as the fencing of coppices, now had to be taken. This had another purpose in addition to securing the wood supply, which was of great interest to our ancestors — providing suitable cover for game; the fallow deer might be reserved for the great lords, but mounted huntsmen and ragged poachers alike enjoyed the pursuit of lesser game.

The commons were difficult to administer. Travellers along the roads that crossed the commons were sometimes prey to thieves, like the luckless Elias le Collier who was robbed of £300 in 1323[13] somewhere near the Beggar's Bush. There was frequent litigation over illegal taking of game in the Chase; by the 15th century this was administered in several parts, Hillwood, Lindridge, Berwood, the Coldfield Walk, for example, each with a Keeper appointed by the Earl of Warwick or his successor. On 24th September 1477 Henry Willoughby of Middleton took a band of 60 men hunting, by permission, in the Hillwood part of the Chase (which extended to Weeford and Hints), but were set upon near Canwell by Lord Lisle of Drayton Bassett, who disputed his right and had mustered over 100 Tamworth men 'arrayed in maner of warre' to ambush him on his way home 'in a long lane fast by Canwell' where 'had not bene the grace of God, thei had bene sleine and distroyed everych one'[14]. Another illegal activity almost certainly occurring in the more remote areas was squatting. At a time of land hunger a district with extensive areas of common land was attractive to homeless people; their labour was in demand, they perhaps had skills which would enrich the life of the community, and they would pay rent to the Lord of the Manor — such people would be allowed to erect a cottage and take in an acre or so of land. On the fringes of the cultivated land, and along the boundaries of the parish, clusters of tiny fields and haphazard cottages were a noticeable feature of the landscape.

1320 has been taken as the high point in the prosperity and intensity of land use in Sutton purely on the basis that the pressure on marginal land can be assumed to have declined from then on. Harvest failure, cattle disease,

27

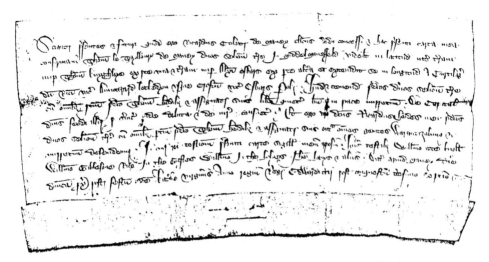

*Charter of 26th November 1363; Richard Colet grants 2 selions of land in
Middle Maney Field to Thomas Taylor
(Birmingham Reference Library Digby 'A' 260(26))*

bubonic plague combined to reduce the population of England to one third of its former numbers by the end of the century[15]. No doubt the feudal system was already in decay by 1320, if it had ever been established in its pure form; between 1363 and 1377 Thomas Taylor of Maney was able to purchase 12 selions of land in Middle Maney Field[16], for which he was to pay the Lord of the Manor in money rather than services. Land ownership was very complicated — the selions or strips of land were scattered over the field, and every other year, when the field was fallow, the cattle and sheep of the whole village grazed freely over the whole field, being folded for the night on a different strip which would thereby be fertilized. However, a farmer with many strips would not only be able to cultivate them in alternate years, but would also be entitled to contribute more animals to the village herd, in proportion to his holdings, thereby gaining extra benefit from the grazing of the commons. This system prevailed in Sutton until at least Elizabethan times, but the decline in prosperity had the effect of converting some of the traditional arable land to permanent pasture (possibly at Wigginshill), the return of some of the assarted marginal land to common, but the retention in cultivation of the more fertile assarts.

Another factor contributing to Sutton's decline was probably a change in attitude of the feudal lord of the manor, the Earl of Warwick. In the changed economic climate the markets and fairs declined and lapsed, the manor house, demesne and park were rented out, and the intention appears to have been to maintain the income from the existing resources so long as the economic climate was unfavourable to expansion. Sir Ralph Bracebridge was the tenant of the manor in 1419, and there is some evidence to suggest that he sought to increase the income from the park by enclosing woodland and developing the fisheries, possibly making Bracebridge Pool, — the annual rent payable was £10 or 120 bream[17]. Some accounts survive for the year 1480, a particularly low ebb in Sutton's fortunes, the Earl of Warwick having been killed in the Wars of the Roses; that year the manor house and its lands had been untenanted, and no-one had rented several of the fisheries and other assets which had previously been profitable — the dove-cote was 'totally broken down and destroyed by crows, and reduced to nothing by rain and wind and other storms'[18]. The net income to King Edward IV, as Lord of the Manor, was £45/12/8 ¾d, but most of this went on salaries and wages for estate officers.

Sutton in 1500 was slowly recovering, although desperately in need of the huge injection of capital which Bishop Vesey was to supply a quarter of a century later. The extensive commons were still subject to forest laws, the hamlets still surrounded by their open fields. Woodland, however, had probably not recovered from being devastated to finance the Earl of Warwick's warlike ambitions, and the area of land under cultivation was still considerably less than it had been in 1320; however, it is not clear how much of the land which was enclosed in the 16th century was the decayed assarts of the earlier period reclaimed, and how much had always been common — Wheatmoor, for example, could equally well be a post-charter (i.e. 16th century) enclosure, or a 13th century assart which survived, or a derelict 13th century assart reclaimed in the 16th Century. Tiny settlements of smallholders with no field system — Four Oaks, Wylde Green, Hill Hook — had survived, embryo nucleated villages which never developed; Hill Hook, which may have begun as an area of extra arable land, or *inhok,* for the village of Hill, would very likely have developed into a proper open field village had not the pattern of agriculture favoured the development of compact enclosed farms in our area after about 1550. The Park was also changing in 1500; at that time the herbage, or income from the grazing rights in the Park, was due to an officer of the King, and over a few decades the income increased considerably; since prices were steady, this may indicate the gradual increase in area of the park from that rented by Sir Ralph Bracebridge to something like the boundaries defined by Bishop Vesey.

Such was the Sutton described by Dugdale: 'the Market being utterly forsaken, the Town fell much to ruin; and the Mannour place was totally pulled down . . . and in this decayed condition did Sutton continue.'[19] Such was the Sutton Vesey found in 1527, and set about transforming it from 'a poor ruinous country place to a flourishing and populous one.'[20]

NOTES

1. SAWYER, P.H. *From Roman Britain to Norman England.* Methuen, 1978, p.148.
2. *Domesday Book — 23 — Warwickshire,* edited by John Morris, Phillimore, 1976.
   See also notes by the present author on the Sutton entry.
3. *Victoria History of the County of Stafford, Vol III, p.214,* edited by M.W. Greenslade, 1970.
4. For an account of Medieval woodland, see RACKHAM, O. *Trees and Woodland in the British Landscape,* Dent 1976.
5. BRACKEN, A.A. *History of the Forest and Chase of Sutton Coldfield,* 1860, P.29.
6. Birmingham Reference Library Deed no. 348038.
7. GELLING, M. *Place-names in the landscape,* Dent 1984, p. 230.
8. HODDER, M. *Earthwork enclosures in Sutton Park,* in Transactions of the Birmingham and Warwickshire Archaeological Society, vol. 89 1978-79, p.166
9. DUGDALE, SIR W. *The Antiquities of Warwickshire,* 2nd ed. 1730, vol. 2 p. 924
10. BERESFORD, M.W. *Lot Acres,* Economic History Review. vol. xii, 1943, p.74-9.
11. BRACKEN, op. cit. p37.
12. *The Beauchamp Cartulary,* Pipe Roll Society vol. 81, 1980.
13. BRACKEN, op. cit. p.38.
14. HISTORICAL MANUSCRIPTS COMMISSION. *Reports on collections no. 69: Lord Middleton.* 1911. p. 116.
15. HATCHER; J. *Plague, population and the English Economy,* Macmillan 1977. p.71.
16. Birmingham Reference Library archives, Digby, A. 258, 260.
17. BRACKEN, op. cit. p.53.
18. *Ministers' Accounts of the Warwickshire Estates of the Duke of Clarence 1479-80,* edited by R.H. Hilton, Dugdale Society Publications vol. XXI 1952.
19. DUGDALE, op.cit. p.913.
20. Sutton Reference Library deed dated 1533.

The Domesday Book Entry for Sutton Coldfield

by Roger Lea

CONTROVERSY RAGES as to the interpretation of almost every part of the Domesday Book record; the following notes are therefore often tentative or inconclusive. The latin text is in italics, the translation in capitals.

Rex Tenet SUTONE. **THE KING HOLDS SUTTON COLDFIELD.** The Warwickshire section of the domesday survey contains over 350 manors, of which 9 were held directly by the Crown, presumably administered locally by a bailiff. (Most of the manors were held by a tenant from a nobleman or bishop, who in turn held it from the king as tenant-in-chief). A reason sometimes given for Sutton being directly held by the king — a royal manor — is that it would have been a valuable headquarters when hunting in the surrounding forest. There is some possibility that its status as a royal manor may have led to the under-recording of its resources — if the survey was made for fiscal purposes the details of the king's direct income would only be of academic interest.

Eduin Comes Tenuit. **EARL EDWIN HELD IT.** Pre-conquest tenure, Edwin, Earl of Mercia, c1063-1070. All his lands were forfeited to the king, but whereas Sutton remained a royal manor, Erdington and Aston were held by William fitz Ansculf (of Dudley) as tenant-in-chief.

Ibi sunt viii hidae et i virgata terrae. **THERE ARE EIGHT HIDES AND ONE VIRGATE OF ARABLE LAND.** A virgate is ¼ of a hide. Feudal dues were based on an assessment of the hidage; a hide originally implied sufficient land to support one family, and is usually reckoned as 120 acres; however it was certainly variable, and in a less fertile area such as Sutton may have been larger. By 1300 a subsistance plot was considered to be ½ virgate or yardland. This assessment appears to indicate at least 1,000 acres of arable land at Sutton Coldfield.

Terra est xxii carucatis. **THERE IS LAND FOR 22 PLOUGHS.** Land for one plough is sometimes considered to be 100 acres, bearing in mind that ⅓ of the land would be autumn-ploughed, $\frac{1}{3}$ spring-ploughed and $\frac{1}{3}$ fallow, and that an acre was approximately a day's work. This would imply twice as much land as the hidage assessment, and an inadequate supply of ploughs (see below).

In dominio est i caruca et ii servi. **IN LORDSHIP THERE IS ONE PLOUGH AND TWO SLAVES.** This is the demesne, the resources of the manor directly controlled by the Lord of the Manor. These resources are modest for a place the size of Sutton, and this reflects the use made of Sutton as an occasional recreational residence where there were other aspects to consider besides the productivity of the land. In some feudal manors the villeins were required to work on the demesne lands for two days a week; in Sutton the customary duties of the villeins related almost entirely to assistance when the Lord came to hunt, leaving no surplus labour available for the cultivation of extensive demesne lands.

Et xx villani. **AND TWENTY VILLAGERS.** The villeins held their lands from the Lord in return for customary services and payments, with the status of serfs, but enjoying some security of tenure and protection, and a few priveleges.

Et iiii bordarii. **AND FOUR SMALLHOLDERS.** There is considerable discussion as to the meaning of the Latin 'Bordar', which seems to indicate a less substantial type of tenant who may have been something like a squatter on the fringes of the village proper.

Under-recording of inhabitants in the forest areas of North Warwickshire and South Staffordshire is proved by comparison with some Burton Abbey charters of the early 12th century, which appear to show that many of the more substantial tenants paid money rents in return for their holdings, and the theory is that they were not mentioned in Domesday Book specifically, but were subsumed under another heading, such as 'value'. A common view is that the average household size was five, so the 26 people mentioned would represent a population of 130 ; on the basis of the Burton Abbey evidence, where there were two money-renters for every villein, this figure could perhaps be trebled, with the possibility of an even higher figure in view of the scattered nature of the settlements and the possible under-recording of a royal manor.

Cum vii carucati. **WITH SEVEN PLOUGHS.** Eight ploughs altogether, but land for 22 ploughs! Some possible explanations:
  (i) Scribal error.
  (ii) Unrecorded tenants may have had unrecorded ploughs. For some
  of the Burton Abbey manors, the ploughlands of the money renters (not

recorded in Domesday Book), added to the Villein's ploughs, equalled the Domesday ploughlands; even assuming a similar pattern for Sutton, with about 45 money-renters with 15 ploughs, we still seem to be thin on the ground compared to those manors, where there were normally 5 or 6 tenants per plough.

(iii) A large proportion of the land may have been left fallow to regain fertility.

(iv) Land may have been lying unused or derelict for some reason.

(v) The light sandy ground may have been very easy to plough.

(vi) It could conceivably reflect an infield/outfield system of agriculture, where a small nucleus of land was in continuous cultivation while a large outer area was cultivated in sections on an occasional basis, each part being ploughed only once or twice in ten years.

x acres prati. **TEN ACRES OF MEADOW.** The size of a Domesday acre is not known, but it was probably similar to the modern measure. Animal husbandry was not very well advanced, and only the best animals would be retained through the winter, being fed on hay, beanstalks etc., the rest being slaughtered at Martinmas (11th November) and salted away.

Silva ii leuugae longitudine et i latitudine. **WOODLAND TWO LEAGUES LONG AND ONE LEAGUE WIDE.** (i) Measurement. The league was of variable size at different places and different times, but 1½ miles has been taken as an informed guess. It is not clear whether the size is that of a single stretch of woodland, or (more likely) the dimensions of several areas of woodland added together. Woods were unlikely to have been perfectly rectangular, and the assumption is that the measurement refers to the length at its longest and the width at its widest. (ii) Definition. Woodland appears to have been of two kinds — coppice woodland intensively managed for the production of all kinds of wood — fencing, fuel, timber for building, tools, charcoal, wagons etc. — and more open woodland available for depasturing animals at various times. Both types were probably present in Sutton, although the deer would have required a good deal of open woodland to roam in.

Cum onerat valet xxx solidi. **WHEN EXPLOITED, VALUE IS THIRTY SHILLINGS.** Literally 'when it bears'. This could refer to the harvesting of timber and wood, or to the value of the acorns for feeding the swine; both of these would be variable, as acorns may be abundant one year and scarce the next.

Totum Manerium valuit et valet iiii librae. **THE VALUE OF THE WHOLE MANOR WAS AND IS FOUR POUNDS.** It is not clear what is included in this figure, which could comprise resources not otherwise recorded such as money rents or income from a mill. Although other entries for royal manors specifically mention mills, the absence of a record does not prove that there was no mill; it may not have been worth recording separately for some reason.

Another notable omission is that no priest is mentioned. In the 12th century the Free Chapel of St. Blaize at the manor house is recorded; a free chapel was outside the normal diocesan jurisdiction, the chaplain being appointed by the lord of the manor directly, so once again the situation is equivocal: if Sutton was served by the clergy of the Free Chapel of St. Blaize in 1086, it is quite possible that such clergy would not figure in Domesday Book, since they would be of the king's household rather than a taxable asset.

The wall between Four Oaks Park and Sutton Park had several gateways to enable the Hartopps and their guests to go driving in Sutton Park; this one, near the railway bridge, has the remains of heraldic deer on the gateposts.

Seeking Signs of Former Times in Sutton Park

HISTORICAL BACKGROUND

by Norman Evans

BEFORE EXPLORING IN THE PARK for evidence of its earlier development, it is necessary to have some knowledge of its historical background.

Sutton Park is the only surviving portion of an extensive hunting ground used by Kings and Earls in Saxon and Norman times and which extended[1] from the present Spaghetti Junction to Barr Beacon and Shenstone. Manor Hill was the site of their hunting lodge which consisted of a Manor House and Chapel[2] within a rectangular area protected by four walls with turrets at each corner.

THE DEER PARK

When Roger, Earl of Warwick, took possession of it in 1126, it is recorded[3] that the manor had a Deer Park with 18 fallow deer. This mention of a reserved area, based on the Manor House, is the earliest indication of an enclosure of a part of the hunting Chase, and recent archaeology has revealed that the Deer Park was of an oval shape extending for just over 2½ miles North of North West from the Manor House. It would appear from the ditch and bank boundaries which still remain that Earl Roger reduced its size to confine the 18 deer within an area based on the Manor and embracing the present Holly Knoll and the lower part of the Keeper's Pool valley, and that some 300 years later this deer park was enlarged on its North side. (see Plan 1.)

Sutton and the hunting ground came into the possession of King Henry VIII, and in 1528, John Harman, a native of Sutton who had risen to become Bishop Vesey of Exeter, persuaded the King to grant a Charter placing the administration of the Royal Town in the hands of a Warden and Society of 24 men (a Mayor and Corporation) and allowing the Bishop to enclose a section of the hunting ground as a Park[4] for the benefit of the inhabitants.

Aerial view of Sutton Park looking over Bracebridge Pool towards Streetly — Bishop Vesey's boundary marks the edge of the residential development.

BISHOP VESEY'S PARK BOUNDARY

The boundary ditch and bank which the Bishop had had constructed can still be traced in places. It enclosed an oval area outlined approximately by the present Monmouth Drive, Chester Road, Thornhill Road, Streetly Lane, Four Oaks Road to the upper end of Hartopp Road, and then in a straight line across the middle of the Four Oaks Estate to the Hartopp end of Ladywood Road. From there it followed the edge of the present Park and along a straight line skirting the Meadow Platt side of Holly Knoll and the Park House grounds, to the present Youth Centre. (Plan 2.)

In Bishop Vesey's time there was no Park Road or Main Entrance as at present, The only way into the Park from the Town being across Wyndley Dam and through the water-splash.

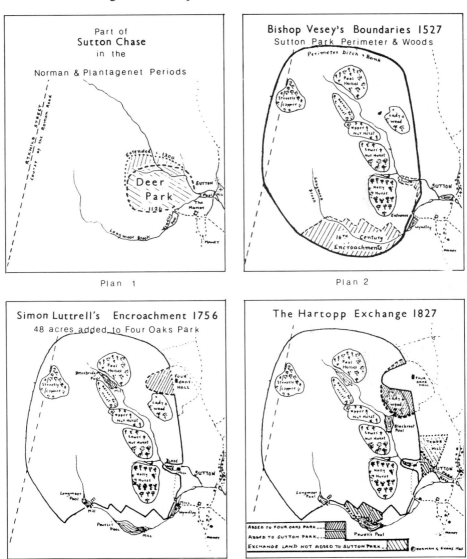

Plans 1 - 4, showing changes in the boundaries and other features of the park

THE 16th CENTURY ENCROACHMENTS

Not long after the death of the Bishop, several irregular encroachments into the Park boundary[5] were made on the Monmouth Drive and Clifton Road side, the most obvious one being the present Park House grounds where a deed dated October 1597 reveals that a water-mill had been built. To reach the Town from this mill, a cutting was made in the hill by the miller's cottage and a cart track was made in a direct line to the Wyndley entrance.

THE FOUR OAKS ENCROACHMENTS

In 1756, Simon Luttrell, who owned Four Oaks Hall, in spite of objections from the Inhabitants of Sutton, evaded the purport of the Charter and obtained an Act of Parliament enabling him to extend his estate[6] by annexing 48 acres of Sutton Park which adjoined it. (See Plan 3).

In 1827, Sir Edmund C. Hartopp, who then owned the Hall, wished to enlarge the 1756 encroachment by taking in another 63 adjoining acres, but was unable to use Simon Luttrell's method because he was prevented by an Injunction from the Court of Chancery which upheld the tenets of the Charter. He was, however, permitted to enter into an exchange of land[7] with the Warden and Society by which he gave them just over 93 acres of land on the Powell's Pool, Meadow Platt and Tudor Hill side of the Park and, to add to his Four Oaks estate received out of the Park 57 acres of the Ladywood plus a strip of 6 acres near the upper end of the present Hartopp Road. (See Plan 4). A condition[8] was imposed, however, that not all of the 93 acres should be added to the Park, but that some should be kept by the Corporation and let on leases for the benefit of the Sutton Charities. The result was that 51½ acres were brought into the Park, i.e. 36½ near Powell's Pool and some 15 acres near the Meadow Platt, the remaining 42 acres on Tudor Hill providing income for the Charities. (See Plan 5).

The main advantage to the inhabitants was that Sir Edmund Hartopp agreed to construct Park Road and a new main entrance to the Park giving easy access for horse-drawn vehicles which had found the old approach via the steep and narrow Wyndley Lane almost impossible.

RESULTING CHANGE OF USES OF THE PARK

Before the Hartopp Exchange of 1827, the Park had been used for its timber, as a pasture for the inhabitants' cattle and for fox hunting, but the new easy access via Park Road soon brought many horse-drawn coach loads[9] of pleasure seeking visitors from further afield, and within 20 years a horse-racing course had been built near Holly Knoll. Subsequently, Sutton's first golf course was constructed between the Main Entrance and Blackroot.

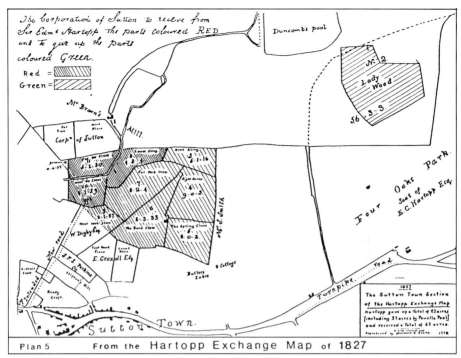

Plan 5 — From the Hartopp Exchange Map of 1827

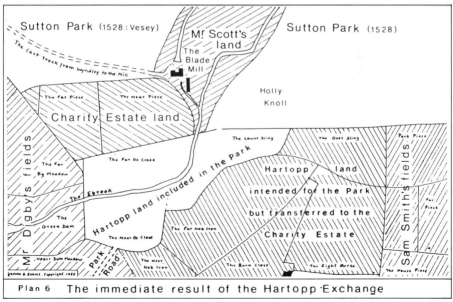

Plan 6 — The immediate result of the Hartopp Exchange

Plans 5 and 6, the Hartopp Exchange (see pp.42-45)

THE EVIDENCE STILL REMAINS

Traces of the Deer park enclosure of 850 years ago and Bishop Vesey's ditch and bank boundaries as well as evidence of the 19th Century activities can still be discovered. The wall marking the Four Oaks park encroachments is well known, and, with knowledge of where to search for man-made alterations to the ground surface, much can be found within a mile of the main Park Road entrance.

Park House (The Blade Mill) as it was in 1870

EXPLORING THE PARK
IN SEARCH OF ITS HISTORY;

Observations on the area between the Main Entrance and Blackroot

WHERE THE TWO BROOKS CONVERGE—THE GREEN DAM

Before entering the park, notice the low-lying ground on which the Park Road flats, the railway embankment and the Gracechurch Shopping Centre have been built; it was formerly a lake about the size of Bracebridge Pool with its dam along the line of the present Parade. This was fed by two streams from the Park. One, from the Longmoor—Wyndley valley entered it near to where the Ebrook flows under the present Clifton Road, and the other, from Bracebridge, entered the lake about half-way between the present Park Road traffic island and the entrance to the Youth Centre.

This was the Mill Pool which supplied the water power for the Town Mill (located near the present Central Library) until on the 24th of July 1668 a disastrous flood[10] broke through the Dams at Wyndley and the Parade and damaged the Town Mill beyond repair.

The Mill Pool was subsequently drained and became a meadow, and later, to help to prevent this becoming flooded, the stream from Bracebridge after crossing the present Meadow Platt was diverted across the upper end of the Mill Pool meadow by constructing a long wide low embankment to lead it to join the Wyndley stream at the small pool by the Youth Centre entrance.

This embankment is marked on the 1824 Corn Rent Map for Sutton as the 'Green Dam',[11] and can still be seen as a long, slightly elevated, very wide grassy bank lying between Clifton Road and the Park opposite Fawdry Close, along the line of which Close it used to flow across the meadow.

This 'Green Dam' has resulted in the height of the stream from the Meadow Platt being slightly above the lowest part of the Old Meadow, and contributes towards the occasional flooding of Fawdry Close and Gerrard Gardens.

HARTOPP EXCHANGE LAND NOT INCLUDED IN THE PARK

Tudor Hill, Richmond Road, the old Midland Railway station and goods yard and the G.P.O. sorting offices occupy the fields which Sir Edmund C. Hartopp handed over to the Town but were never included in the Park, the income from them being applied to the Sutton Charities. This came about because in 1792 the Corporation had neglected to carry out the tenets of the Royal Charter which Bishop Vesey had intended should help the poorest inhabitants of Sutton. Since that date, the Corporation had had to obtain the approval of all its transactions by a Master in the Court of Chancery[12], who decreed that any exchange of land with Sir Edmund must be to the benefit of the poor. He therefore asked the Bishop of Lichfield to hold a clerical inquiry to determine by what means this could be accomplished, and subsequently approved the decision that 42 acres given by Sir Edmund in the Tudor Hill area should not be annexed to the Park, but[13] that the income from that land should be used to augment the Sutton Charities.

The Eastern boundary[14] of those fields was the water-course which can still be seen half-way along the footpath which connects Richmond Road with Clifton Road, and extended up towards Mulroy House in Mulroy Road. From there, the area was bounded on the North by a field hedge along a straight line to the Park, its position to-day being marked by the limit of the built-up area.

The boundary between those Tudor Hill fields and the Meadow Platt follows the line of an original field hedge thus accounting for its irregular shape, but to appreciate the changes which have taken place within the Park near the Town Gate, older boundaries there must be sought out, and former fields discovered and named by reference to the Warden and Society minute books and contemporary maps and plans.

THE ORIGINAL FIELDS IN THE PARK

On entering the Park from Park Road, it should be appreciated that — except for Holly Knoll in the distance and land in the Wyndley direction — no part of the original Park given by the Charter of King Henry VIII in 1528 can be seen from here, and that all the present Park near the Town Gate has been added between 1828 and 1830, and was formerly a small part of the land farmed by Mr George Brown, the miller, from the Blade Mill which adjoined the present Park House.

This part of the Park which is visible from the Main Entrance consisted of five fields. (See Plan 5).

The field on the right, now known as the Meadow Platt, was then called the Lower Sling[15] and extended as far as the base of Holly Knoll where, at the line of oak trees, it adjoined the original 1528 Park.

On the left of the Entrance in the direction of the Youth Centre were four fields, the one between the public conveniences and the brook was called the Near Ox Close[16], and one just across the stream was called the Far Ox Close[17] __ on part of which the children's paddling pool has been constructed. The far boundary of this latter Close has been obliterated, but its position can be determined by following the original 1528 Park boundary from the remains of the small quarry with its pine trees on the Meadow Platt side of Holly Knoll, along the line of oak trees (4 remain) towards the gate of the park House and continuing in a straight line along traces of an old boundary bank to the clump of trees near the Youth Centre building.

From here, to the South West of this old Far Ox Close, the land rises up towards the cross-roads and the road leading to the Wyndley Entrance. Almost parallel with and on the Town side of this road are the remnants of a line of holly bushes which were part of the upper hedge boundary of two fields extending from the Youth Centre fence to the drive immediately in front of the Park House and bounded by the Far Ox Close on the Town side. The field adjacent to the Park House was called the Near Piece[18] and part of it is still seen as the grassy hill overlooking the front of that building, while the other field, called the Far Piece[19], occupied the space between the Near Piece and the Youth Centre fence and now contains the new Park Information Centre.

THE IMMEDIATE RESULT OF THE HARTOPP EXCHANGE (see plan 6)

Sir Edmund Hartopp, in order to extend his Four Oaks Hall estate, had bought nine fields on the Town side of the Park from Wriothesley Digby, Esquire and offered them (together with similarly acquired land adjoining Powell's Pool) in exchange for Lady Wood which at that time was within Sutton Park. Of the nine fields, only three, namely the Near Ox Close, the Far Ox Close and the Lower Sling (i.e. the Meadow Platt) were actually added on the Town side to the 1528 Park, the new and only access to which — resulting from the Exchange — was limited to crossing the short boundary at the line of oak trees at the far end of the Meadow Platt.

A study of the Corn Rent and the Hartopp Exchange maps will show that at that time there was no possibility of making a road from the Town Gate towards the Wyndley entrance as such a route was completely blocked by the Far Piece and Near Piece fields and the Blade Mill grounds and pool. (See Plan 6). It will also be seen from the Exchange map and by observation on the ground that Park Road (which had been built and paid for by Sir Edmund Hartopp) had been laid in such a direction that if it had been continued across the Meadow Platt in a straight line it would have entered the 1528 Park at the base of Holly Knoll and that the building of a bridge over the stream would have been avoided.

BLADE MILL GROUNDS NEGOTIATIONS

In March 1828, Mr John Scott who owned the Blade Mill and its land and pool upstream wrote[20] to the Warden and Society asking for the Near Piece and Far Piece fields to be included in the Blade Mill estate, and in exchange offered an equivalent amount of land in another part of Sutton.

The Warden and Society were the owners of those two fields, and although they were part of the Charity Estates were considering making an alternative road across them to join the Town Gate to the Wyndley entrance. Realising that Mr Scott was amenable to an exchange of land and that an alternative route for a road could be obtained by acquiring the Blade Mill and grounds, they deliberated on this possibility for just over twelve months, and in April 1929 proposed to Mr Scott[21] that they should take over those grounds and offered him in exchange an equal value of land in Sutton. Mr Scott resented this reversal of his suggestion and would not consider giving up the Blade Mill and its land, so the Warden and Society made him a new proposition[22] of exchange of land and offered him part of the Near Piece field on the conditions that he 'build a bridge over the brook, make a road round the land which Mr Scott is to receive in exchange, and also be subject to all expenses arising from fencing or otherwise'.

As Mr Scott would not agree to the Corporation's conditions which would have made him construct the road and bridge for them, a compromise was reached in May 1829 by which they incorporated the Far Piece and part of the Near Piece into the Park, made the present road over the stream and across the Near Piece, and in an exchange of land gave Mr Scott about half of the Near Piece field. This accounts for the grassy hill facing the present frontage of the Park House being included within those grounds — that estate remaining in private possession until bought[23] by the Sutton Corporation in 1948 for £19,250.

Sir Edmund Hartopp shared[24] the cost of the new 400 yards of road from the Town Gate to its junction with the old road which extended from Wyndley entrance close to the upper boundary of the Far and Near Pieces and descended to the Blade Mill, and also the cost of the bridge which was described in the Minutes[25] as carrying a road supported by a brick arch 9 inches thick, 30 feet in length and 4 feet in span. The estimated cost of its construction was £60. The present bridge was built in 1947.

The road and boundary changes resulting from the Hartopp Exchange and the subsequent negotiations thus account for the road from the Town bending to the left on entering the Park, and for the Park House continuing in private possession.

ANCIENT CUSTOMS UPHELD

The fact that the Meadow Platt and the Near and Far Ox Closes adjoining the stream were not part of the Park given to the Town under King Henry VIII's Charter in 1528 meant that any visiting circuses, fun fairs or similar static events could make temporary use of these areas without infringement of the principles of the Charter which gave the inhabitants uninterrupted Rights of Common and access at all times to all parts of the 1528 Park.

This gave rise to the custom of confining such temporary events to these three 'Hartopp exchange' fields near the Town Gate and the three fields adjoining Powell's Pool which were also added to the park by the Hartopp Exchange.

THE OLD ROAD TO THE BLADE MILL

The stream flowing down the valley by the present Park House had been dammed across to provide water-power for the Mill at the time of the 1597 encroachment. Neither the Pool nor the Mill remain, but the original cart road from the Mill can still be found, much overgrown, leading from the cottages by the Park House up the steep cutting in the direction of the Wyndley entrance. The steepness of this climb (gradient 1 in 4½) for horses and wagons implies that the Near Piece and the Far Piece must have been encroachments into the Park earlier than 1597 and were already in occupation, otherwise the builder of the first Mill there would have included the land occupied by the Near and Far Pieces in his own encroachment and thus obtained a very much easier gradient for his horse-drawn wagons round the edge of the hill. The only route for these loads from the Mill to Sutton Town before the Exchange was up this 1 in 4½ hill and onwards along the road to the Wyndley entrance, across the Dam and up the steep Wyndley Lane (gradient 1 in 7) to descend into Sutton by the side of the Cup Inn; so the negotiations of 1829 rewarded Mr Scott and Mr Brown, his miller, with the advantage of an almost level access along Park Road to the Town and only a quarter of the former distance to travel.

THE ANCIENT DEER PARKS WITHIN SUTTON PARK

When, in 1126, Roger, Earl of Warwick, exchanged his two Manors in Rutland to obtain possession of the Manor at Sutton, it was recorded that he and his heirs would obtain the Sutton Manor together with one Park enclosing 18 fallow deer. This Deer Park was contained within a boundary which consisted of a ditch and a bank with a fence on it of sufficient depth and height to prevent deer from jumping up from the ditch (which was on the Deer Park side) over the elevated fence to escape on to the Sutton Chase beyond. Over the centuries the banks have become eroded and the ditches have lost their depth but are still traceable.

The location of these ditch and bank boundaries within Sutton Park, and subsequent 12th and 14th century alterations were discovered in 1978 by Michael A. Hodder, B.A. whose research is recorded in the Transactions of the Birmingham and Warwickshire Archaeological Society, Vol 89, and in his 'Sutton Coldfield, an Archaeological Survey'; both of which works can be studied in the Sutton Local History Reference Library.

LOCATING THE 12th CENTURY DEER PARK BOUNDARY

On the North side of Holly Knoll can be found traces of the boundary of the 12th century Deer Park which was oval in shape and extended from the Manor House on Manor Hill to just above Keeper's Well, part of the bank and ditch which circumscribed this Deer Park can be found by ascending the steep path rising from the clump of pine trees at the end of the Meadow Platt and searching in the holly bushes which edge the North side of Holly Knoll at the top of the climb. The ditch is on the Manor Hill side of the bank. This boundary extends from here in a West direction towards the three-arch brick bridge which crosses over the stream coming from Blackroot Pool, and its bank would have provided a causeway across the boggy valley and to Lower Nut Hurst wood beyond. The Warden and Society Minutes record that there were stepping stones in the water there in 1742, the brick bridge (recently restored) being of later Georgian origin.

This Deer Park boundary passes through Lower Nut Hurst above Keeper's Pool quarry and emerges from the wood just above Keeper's Well. On the West side of Holly Hurst it merges with Bishop Vesey's ditch and bank boundary of that wood but can be distinguished from the latter by a study of the relative position of the ditch and bank. The wood has its boundary ditch on the outside of its bank, thus preventing animals from entering the wood to damage it, but the Deer Park has its ditch on the inside of its boundary to prevent deer escaping on to the Sutton Chase.

THE 12th CENTURY DEER PARK ENLARGED

Around 1298, Guy, Earl of Warwick[26], developed Sutton as a Town with its Parish Church, established a market, and is believed to have been responsible for the enlargement of the Deer Park in the direction of the present Blackroot Pool.

The boundary of this larger Deer Park can be much more easily traced than the former one, and from the Northern side of Holly Knoll can be followed for nearly a mile across the lower Blackroot valley to the far side of the Lower Nut Hurst wood.

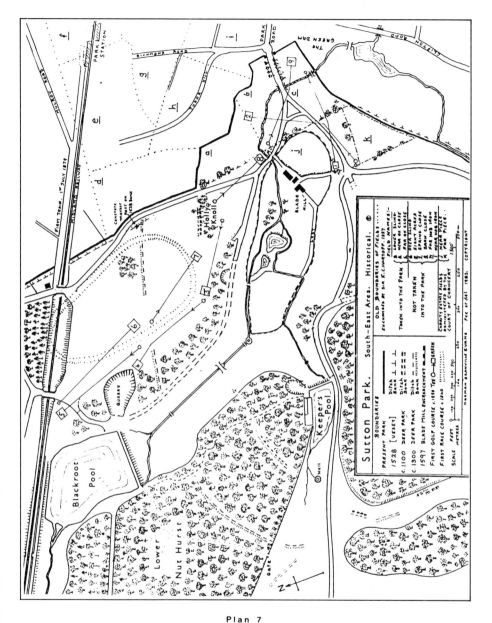

Plan 7

Signs of former times: map of the South-eastern corner of the Park

LOCATING THE ENLARGED DEER PARK BOUNDARY

Starting from the clump of pine trees in the former small quarry at the side of Holly Knoll adjoining the Meadow Platt, the boundary of the enlarged Deer Park can be found by walking up the motor road in the direction of the Hartopp Gate entrance. This road, ascending up the hill, bends a little to the left, and at the upper end of this curve a modern small concrete post bearing the words 'Electric Cables' will be seen in the grass on the left 23 feet (7 metres) from the edge of the motor road. Walk 90 feet (27½m) from the concrete post towards Holly Knoll along a slight bank (covering the cables). Turn right and cross the old Race Course track (here in a shallow cutting) to observe the 14th century bank and ditch (the ditch is on the Manor side) which continues directly ahead and can be followed to the motor road just below Blackroot. The ditch and bank have become eroded in the valley below Blackroot Dam and on the land rising up into Lower Nut Hurst wood, but can be seen again very easily in the Keeper's Valley part of that wood.

This part of the 14th century boundary can be found from the motor road above Keeper's Pool by looking for a five-bar field gate in the fencing of Lower Nut Hurst, about 250 yards (230m.) up the hill from Keeper's Well. The distance from the centre of this gate in the direction of Keeper's Pool to the top of the Deer Park bank is 132 feet (40m.) and both bank and ditch are well defined within the wood.

The Deer Park boundary can be traced in places where it crosses Keeper's Valley and can be seen again between Holly Hurst wood and the New Plantation. Up the hill at the edge of Holly Hurst it will be found to merge with the banks and ditches of the earlier Deer Park boundary, and with Bishop Vesey's boundary of Holly Hurst as mentioned above.

THE FIRST RACECOURSE

The first Racecourse in Sutton Park occupied the area between Holly Knoll and the Railway cutting. (See Plan 7.) It was in use[27] in the second half of the 1840's and it has been reported that the Birmingham Races were held there in 1847. Although all traces of the track have disappeared from the open ground between Blackroot quarry and the Hartopp Road railway bridge, it can still be seen clearly where it curves through a cutting in the North part of Holly Knoll. From here it can be followed close to the motor road in the direction of the railway bridge and, according to the Corporation minutes of 18th March 1878, extended over the present railway cutting between the two road bridges before curving towards Blackroot quarry. A second, and much larger, racecourse was subsequently constructed in the Longmoor Valley adjoining Westwood Coppice.

Aerial view looking west from Town Gate, showing the area covered by plan 7; note the avenues of trees planted on various special occasions.

Tree-planting ceremony in Sutton Park, Queen Victoria's Golden Jubillee, 1887

THE FIRST GOLF LINKS

A more leisurely pastime was introduced into the Park circa 1880 by the then Rector of Sutton Coldfield, the Rev. W.K. Riland Bedford, when he supervised the construction of the first Sutton Golf Links.

This original course[28] — before any links were made near Streetly — was in the region of the Meadow Platt, Holly Knoll and the plateau above Blackroot quarry, and consisted of 9 holes starting and finishing near the present Town Gate. Some of the greens can still be found with the assistance of a plan which is in the possession of the Sutton Coldfield Golf Club at Streetly, and from which details are reproduced here. (See Plan 7.)

The first tee was by the footbridge near the present children's paddling pool, and its green 320 yards away is easily found on the Town Gate side of the group of holly bushes at the cross-roads where the motor road to Keeper's Pool branches from the road which joins the Town Gate to the Wyndley entrance. It is a flat green close to the Park House field, and its bunker by the field hedge is obvious even after 100 years.

The golfers then returned down the hill and crossed the brook to the second green which was located near the middle of the Meadow Platt

50

opposite the present Park House entrance. From here they proceeded towards Blackroot keeping Holly Knoll on their right and continued on across the plateau above Blackroot quarry to the far side of the motor road by the railway bridge near Blackroot car park. Here was the 5th green, the furthermost part of the course. Their return followed much the same route but in a more direct line to the top of Holly Knoll.

The 8th green — not difficult to find — was a 160 yard drive down from Holly Knoll, and can still be seen as a flat square elevated area of grass located at the Holly Knoll side of the brook and at the edge of the road where the stream emerges from under the road bridge near the Park House gate.

KING GEORGE V CORONATION AVENUE

Bordering the main road in the Park at the Town Gate are a few trees which are the remnants of an avenue of 28 lime trees extending in the Blackroot direction. They were planted on 23rd June 1911 as part of the celebrations[29] in Sutton to commemorate the Coronation of King George V. The first two trees were planted by the Mayor, Councillor T.H. Cartwright and the Mayoress, Mrs Cartwright, and the other 26 by the wives of the Sutton Councillors. Each lady received a silver spade suitably inscribed as a souvenir of the occasion.

THE CATTLE PENS *

Just inside the Town Gate entrance on the left, beyond the public conveniences, will be seen the pens in which cattle were placed for identification marking before being put to graze in the Park. This is now done by means of a numbered tag fixed to an ear, but until recently each animal was branded on a hoof, the hot irons painlessly indenting the letters 'S.P.' (Sutton Park) followed by a number.

SUTTON PARK—A WATER CATCHMENT AREA

It should be observed that although a considerable amount of water flows along the Eachelhurst Valley at Walmley leaving Sutton near the former Plant's Mill to become a tributary of the River Tame, no stream enters the Sutton boundaries, and that most of this water accumulates within the catchment area of Sutton Park itself, through which it flows in the valleys either from Longmoor or from Bracebridge.

These streams form the Ebrook, the name by which the brook through Sutton is recorded in all manuscript records of previous centuries, the earliest known entry of that name being in 1287 when the Earl of Warwick granted Thomas de Arden of Peddimore Hall permission to fish 'in that little stream called Ebrook'[30].

Removed in 1989.

The name 'Plants Brook' arose after 1875 when the Birmingham, Tame and Rea drainage scheme was being planned at Minworth. The short length of the Ebrook, from Kingsbury Road to its confluence with the River Tame, was known there by the name of a former miller, Mr Plant, whose mill was close to the present canal. The drainage surveyors recorded Mr Plant's stream through his fields as 'Plant's' brook, and to avoid having two names for the same flow of water and for the convenience of the plans being prepared, regarded all the waters entering the system from Sutton as being from 'Plants' brook — a substituted name unfamiliar to the old Warden and Society and the inhabitants of Sutton Coldfield.

Crowds of people flocking to Sutton Park c. 1910 along Park Road (p.38)

Sources of Information

A. Dugdale. Antiquities of Warwickshire. 1730 Edition.
B. Bracken. History of the Forest and Chase of Sutton Coldfield.
C. King Henry VIII's Charter for Sutton Coldfield. 1528.
D. Charity Estate Plans for Sutton, 1811.
E. Corn Rent Map of Sutton Coldfield, 1824.
F. Hartopp Exchange Map, 1827.
G. Warden and Society Minute Books.
H. Warden and Society Committee Minute Book 1828—1838.
J. Sutton Coldfield Parish Church Registers.
K. Sutton Coldfield Golf Club Records.
L. King George V Coronation Celebrations Handbook, 1911.
M. Birmingham & Warwickshire Archaeological Society Transactions, 1978/79. p. 166.
N. Deeds of the Park House.

References

No.	Above Source	No.	Above Source
1.	A. Page 910	17.	F.
2.	B. Page 52.	18.	D.
3.	B. Page 28.	19.	D.
4.	C.	20.	H. Minutes 8th March 1828.
5.	E.	21.	G. Minutes 10th April 1829.
6.	B. Page 92.	22.	G. Minutes 1st May 1829.
7.	F.	23.	N.
8.	G. Minutes 8th March 1828	24.	G. Minutes 5th Nov. 1828.
9.	H.	25.	H. Minutes 2nd May 1829.
10.	J. 1668	26.	A. Page 911.
11.	E.	27.	G. Minutes 13th Aug. 1849.
12.	G. Minutes 16th May 1792.	28.	K.
13.	H. Minutes 8th March 1828.	29.	L.
14.	F.	30.	B. Page 108.
15.	F.		
16.	F.		

Parish Church and Trinity Hill, c1800, (Aylesford Collection)

Parish Church and Trinity Hill, 1988

Holy Trinity Parish Church, Sutton Coldfield

By Andrew MacFarlane

THE ENGLISH PARISH CHURCH stands as the one building which has been everywhere cherished, extended, adapted, and continuously used over many centuries. It provides a direct link with people of the past, and is a repository and showcase for their names, memories, wealth and skills.

Sutton Coldfield Parish Church is no exception. For nearly 700 years it has been a centre of worship, and a focal point for the people of the town throughout that time. Although W.K. Riland Bedford wrote of the building that 'solidity and plainness' are its main characteristics, it nevertheless displays fine examples of sculpture, architecture, furnishing and decoration; it holds numerous clues to the lives and works of Suttonians long dead.

Until the Church was built, Sutton was served by the Chapel of St. Blaise at the Manor House, but with the expansion of the town in the 13th century this was no longer appropriate. Although the precise date of building is unknown, it was probably about 1280; the first record of it is in 1291, and the market charter of 1300 specified Holy Trinity Eve as fair day.

There have been five periods of major building works on the church. The original building was a simple nave and chancel built from the local red sandstone; the only part of this still to be seen is at the base of the chancel wall next to Coleshill Street. The style of the exterior is probably similar to the original, particularly in the arches of the windows, which have the characteristic geometrical tracery of the early 14th century, with attractive flowered carving in the upper pointed arches. This early church remained unchanged for over a century, but sometime in the middle of the fourteenth century the tower was built; similar building was accomplished at that time at the parish churches of Yardley, Sheldon, and Kings Norton.

When Bishop Vesey settled in Sutton and set about transforming it into a prosperous town, he naturally turned his attention to the church. He added the South and North Aisles and the Chapel which bears his name and

The plinth at the base of the Chancel wall, which can be seen from Coleshill Street, is the oldest surviving stonework, dating in part to the original building of c.1290.

contains his tomb; the size of the church was more than doubled; the original exterior north and south walls of the nave were replaced by large Romanesque arches. These arches are supposed to be imitations of some that Vesey had admired in Paris, which he had visited in his diplomatic travels. In the design of the north and south exterior walls, he remained loyal to the style of the original windows. Vesey increased the number of bells, installed the first organ, and almost certainly added the porch. The rôle of the porch in parish churches was considerable, as an area between the spiritual and secular worlds. Commercial deals were often struck here, and it was customary for sinners to confess serious misdemeanours in the porch before being admitted back into the Church and to the sacraments.

During Vesey's time, chantries were suppressed. One had existed at the Parish Church, founded by one Thomas Broadmeadow, who had left funds for a priest to sing mass and pray for the souls of himself and his family. No further notable building seems to have taken place until the 18th century, when the Corporation of Sutton Coldfield several times made large payments for restoration and rebuilding.

Between 1739 and 1749, there were considerable repairs to the roof, and in 1759 there was a major rebuilding which followed the collapse of the nave. The anonymous author of a history of the town wrote in 1762 that the nave was 'lately taken down and rebuilt with a sort of hard sandstone of which there is a plentiful quarry within half a mile'. The writer described the addition of a wooden gallery in the South Aisle, and mentioned the installation of a chiming clock 'newly put up by an approved artist . . . from the neighbouring town of Birmingham'. The Corporation later paid out 100 guineas to renew the church bells, the work being carried out by Chapman, Mears and Company, Bell-Founders, of Whitechapel, London. These were unsatisfactory, and the same firm replaced them a few years later.

In the 19th century, the rapid growth of the town led to the division of the parish, with the building of three other churches, but it was still necessary to increase the size of Holy Trinity by further extensions to the building. The outer North Aisles and the Clergy Vestry were added between 1874 and 1879, remaining faithful in style to the older buildings. The roof level of the nave was raised. In the Holbeche Diary we read of the author's disapproval of 'the peaked roof of the nave which from the outside dwarfs the noble tower'. The bells were recast, and two more added in 1883. In the present century, more attention has quite rightly been spent on preservation, and some noteworthy work has been carried out. The strikingly attractive decoration of the chancel roof was accomplished in 1914, and the roof of the Vesey Chapel in 1929. The Choir Vestry was built in the north-west corner.

Inside the church there are a number of particularly noteworthy items, the most ancient of which is the sandstone font. This is older than the church itself, dating from 1100-25, and contains 21 carved panels made by intersections between carved Norman arches; four large grotesque corbel heads glare out from the rim. The font was in use as a horse mounting block at Shustoke in the 19th century, having been discarded from Over Whitacre Church during restorations, when it was discovered by Richard Sadler. The Sadler family had legal and business interests in Sutton Coldfield, and the font was for years used as a garden ornament behind their premises in High Street, until they presented it to Holy Trinity Church.

Another antique item is the misericord with its carving of grapes being stolen from a vineyard. The choir screens between the Chancel and the Vesey Chapel are also carved from oak, and date from the early 17th century. They were originally housed in Worcester Cathedral, but were discarded during renovations; they were purchased by the Rector of Sutton at the time, W.K. Riland Bedford, and brought to the church. He also obtained the tower archway screens from Valetta in Malta, where he had strong personal links. The pulpit dates from the rebuilding of the nave in 1759-60.

Holy Trinity Church ·· Sutton Coldfield.

Enlargements of the Church.

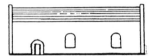

Figure 1

By 1300   There was a church on Trinity Hill consisting only of a chancel and small nave.

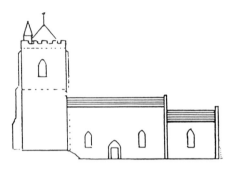

Fig. 2

By 1500   The tower had been built and the nave extended and joined up with it.

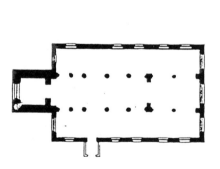

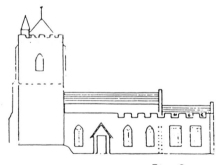

Fig. 3

By 1533   Bishop Vesey had widened the church by building two side-aisles and provided an organ and four bells.

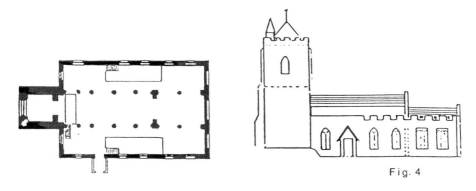

Fig. 4

By 1740   Three small galleries had been built, one over each side - aisle and one across the West end of the nave.

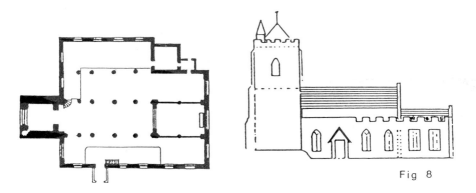

Fig 8

By 1880   The church had been widened on the North side, the 1760 galleries (except the South one) removed, and a larger one built over the new North aisle. The West arch of the nave had been re-opened and the external doorway to the tower stone stairs blocked up. The pulpit had been moved to the nave from the chancel, the floor of which had been raised to accommodate the choir stalls – built with oak from Worcester Cathedral. New pews had been erected throughout the church, except in the South gallery which remains unaltered.

Plans of the church at various times. The elevations show that, although the increased height of the nave by 1880 is only slight, the visual effect is dramatic enough to justify Holbeche's complaint (p.57)

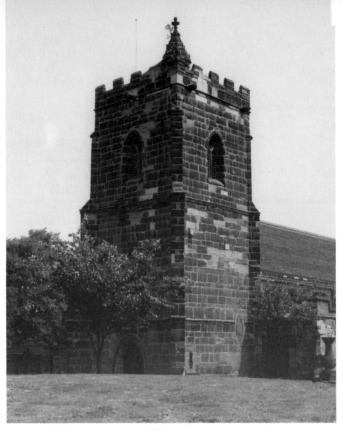

The tower

The Vesey Chapel contains the most noteworthy of the Church's monuments. The stained-glass windows are modern, each of the four arches depicting a bishop associated with Sutton Coldfield. From left to right, these are as follows: 1. John Arundel, Rector of Sutton in 1431, later Bishop of Chichester; ii. Bishop Vesey; iii. Bishop Hacket of Lichfield, whose family lived at Moor Hall and Moxhull Hall; iv. Dr. Fleetwood, Bishop of Worcester after the Restoration, who was appointed Rector in 1642, but never took up the appointment owing to the Civil War.

The tomb of Bishop Vesey is the church's one monument of national renown; the effigy of Vesey was reputedly sculpted from life, and is the only example of a bishop dressed in pre-Reformation robes. The monument is a worthy tribute to the memory of an extraordinary Tudor statesman, whose later years were devoted to an almost unique experiment in town planning in his native Sutton. In the century after Vesey's death, Sutton was a centre of stern puritanism; it is no small tribute to Vesey's memory that his tomb was not desecrated as a relic of romanism. The tomb has been restored on a number of occasions; the accounts still exist of the 1742 work of 'repairing and beautifying ye Bishop's Monument', and in 1875, when a further restoration took place, the opportunity was taken to open the tomb. Members of the Corporation attended the opening, and were disappointed at the lack of relics within. The tomb was filled with dry sand, amid which were found the upper part of a skull, a jaw-bone containing two teeth of great age, and some fragments of bone; there was no trace of the lead-lined coffin, the ecclesiastical rings, and other items which would have been interred with the bishop. Clearly the tomb had been opened at some time in the past. The remains were placed in an earthenware vase, those present signed a parchment which described the occasion and this was put in a bottle which was sealed with the vase inside the tomb.

The other particularly striking monument in the chapel is the Pudsey Memorial, set in the north wall. This was designed and executed by William Wilson, the local architect and sculptor who had been a pupil of Sir Christopher Wren; he was knighted by Charles II and married Jane, the

The font

The Vesey Chapel as it was in 1895, showing the window of the four bishops, Vesey's Tomb in the corner, and the Pudsey Monument on the left.

widow of Henry Pudsey of Langley Hall. He built Moat House, allegedly so that she could live in the style she was used to. Before his death, Wilson expressed the wish to be buried alongside his wife, under the monument which he had designed. Family opposition from the Pudseys prevented this, and he was buried close by in the churchyard adjacent to the north wall of the Vesey Chapel. He had taken the refusal of his request philosophically, saying "I will be buried on the outside of the church, directly opposite the vault where my wife lies, and there will be only a single stone wall between us: and as I am a stonemason, there will be no kind of labour or difficulty in cutting my road through the wall to my old bedfellow". With the building of the Clergy Vestry in the 19th century, it seemed Wilson's prediction had borne fruit, as his grave was now inside the church.

Numerous memorials inside and outside the church give indications of the Rectors who have led the local congregations over nearly 700 years. Although Rectors were under the authority of the Bishop, they were appointed on the recommendation of the owners of the advowson of the parish. The advowson, or living, originally belonged to the Lords of the Manor; in 1291 this was the Earl of Warwick, and the value of the living was 20 marks (£13.33p). Although there are earlier records of a priest at

Sutton, Gregory Harold is supposed to have been the first Rector, in 1305. Not much is known of the early Rectors, except John Arundel, Rector from 1431-2, later Bishop of Chichester and physician to Henry VI.

In 1504 the Rector was John Taylor, a prolific author, who became Ambassador to Burgundy and Clerk to Parliament in 1509, possibly on the recommendation of Vesey. Taylor was the first-born of triplets, whose infant heads are depicted in a monument at Barton-under-Needwood Church. Ralph Wendon remained rector through the turbulent years of Henry VIII's breach with the Pope, the protestant reformation of Edward VI, the return of England to Roman Catholicism under Mary Tudor, and Elizabeth I's accession. Since 1470, the living had belonged to the Crown, but in 1559 it was sold to Thomas Gibbons of New Hall, with all its 'Rectory, woods, underwoods and trees'. He sold it for £100 in 1586 to Thomas Shilton, a mercer of Birmingham, thus beginning a family connection which lasted for over 300 years.

It is safe to assume that Shilton held vigorous puritan opinions, shared by the parishioners of Sutton Coldfield. A significant appointment as Rector was John Burges, who had refused to wear a surplice in 1590 and offended James I by preaching a puritan sermon before him, getting a prison sentence in the Fleet Prison and being deprived of his church living for a time. In 1517 he was doctor and chaplain to English protestant troops fighting for Frederick of Bohemia in the 30 years war; on his return to England he became Rector of Sutton.

Antony Burges, not related to John, but holding similarly energetic puritan opinions, was Rector during the turbulent years of the Civil War, and until the Restoration. He was a figure of some note, being called to preach before the Houses of Parliament, and under the Commonwealth, was appointed Commissioner for Warwickshire, charged with the 'ejection of scandalous, ignorant and insufficient ministers and schoolmasters'. He fled from Sutton at one time, seeking safety in London, returning about 1650 when the area was firmly under Parliamentary control; the Parish Register says 'there was baptized the 23rd of June a child of Mr Antony Burges named Philip'. Unable to subscribe to the Act of Conformity, he retired to Tamworth in 1662, and died in 1664.

The old rectory (nos. 1,3 and 5 Coleshill Street) opposite the church was valued at £120 in 1671, more than Moor Hall or New Hall, and the same as Langley Hall. John Riland was Rector in 1701, having purchased the living from his Shilton relatives, and he built a new rectory, a grand mansion of brick, in the Queen Anne style to a design, probably, of William Wilson, and set in the pleasant surroundings of Rectory Park; it cost £239.11s.3d.

The Queen Anne Rectory

The nonconformity so pronounced in the early 1600s was now reversed; John Riland was a high churchman, a staunch tory, and openly showed his Jacobite sympathies. He attended meetings at Coleshill at which toasts were drunk to the 'White Rose' (the emblem of James Stuart, the Old Pretender); most of the local gentry were of the same mind.

The Riland family appear to have accepted the Hanoverian monarchy by mid-century (John Riland had written of George I 'an unlearned king was a crowned ass . . . if so, what is our K. George?'). Deep concern was shown as Bonnie Prince Charlie's army advanced towards Derby in 1745, and the family silver was submerged in an ornamental canal at the Rectory to prevent its capture by the Jacobites.

The conflict between the roles of Pastor and landowner were exposed after Richard Bisse Riland became Rector in 1758. Although he was described as "an ornament and an honour to the clerical profession", he was involved in contentious issues. The newly repaired church brought accusations that the Rector was fomenting "private discontents" and "parochial dissensions", especially when in 1760 the quarrels were about the allocation of seating in the new church pews. A corporation minute of 1763 begins "Whereas several greedy people of low rank, intending to take for themselves some of the best seats in this Parish Church. . .", and it was resolved to allocate the pews on the same basis as before. An official plan was made, showing which seats were reserved for particular households, for example, "North side of the Middle Aisle — The Warden, The Parsonage, Charles Sacheverell".

A proposal was made in 1778 to enclose the commons, the resulting fields to be allocated to inhabitants. This proposal included the Park, and favoured local landowners against the small farmers and cottagers; the Rector owned a great deal of land — he would have received 1/7th of the Park, for example, — and he actively supported the proposal; the townspeople rallied against it, however, and it was defeated with acrimony.

R.B. Riland died in 1790 and was followed by his brother John, who, although elderly, showed energy and devotion to his parish affairs which seems to contrast with his predecessor. He was noted for his frequent visits on foot to parishioners, often walking for many miles. He urged the use of local funds to establish elementary schools, and Sunday schools were established in 1806 for girls, and in 1811 for boys. Increasingly aged and inform, there is a description of his wig catching fire as he bent too low over the candles in church.

The subsequent Rector, William Riland Bedford, died from apoplexy in a Birmingham street in 1843, and his son, William Kirkpatrick Riland Bedford, became Rector in 1850. He served for over 40 years, and in his

Canon W.C. Riland Bedford

intellect, and wide-ranging interests, showed the characteristics of a learned, concerned and prosperous Victorian gentleman. He travelled widely; Holbeche noted that he was absent a great deal, and that Mr Packwood preached instead: "He has a monotonous, soothing voice" and "we frequently got into trouble for sleeping". He was interested in cricket, and helped to found the "Free Foresters", many of whose early games were played in Rectory Park. Another of his interests was local history, publishing "300 Years of a family Living", on his family's connection with the Rectory, in 1889, and the *History of Sutton Coldfield,* a devoted and scholarly work which is still quite unsurpassed, in 1891.

Some of the light-hearted comments from the Holbeche Diary give a flavour of the church in the 1860s:

—"ours was a long pew and so was the service"

—"The organist, Mr Lampert, played flourishes on the organ as curly as a pig's tail"

—George Brentnell "occupied a tiny square pew . . and sometimes had a dog on his lap".

—The Perkins (of Moat House) had a pew "in what might pass for a square room in the Bishop's Monument".

—"Blue Coat School" boys sat in tiers in the church while "one-legged Mr Felton administered knocks to their heads".

—the Hartopps of Four Oaks Hall entered the church "always when the psalms were being read . . . in single file . . . and passed with ridiculous dignity . . . verily there are snobs of every degree".

W.K. Riland Bedford died in 1892, and was succeeded by his son, Canon W. C. Riland Bedford, the last incumbent from this long family connection. In 1907, the Sutton Coldfield Rectory Act was passed, designed to remove from the Riland Bedford family the right to combine the ownership of the living with the office of Rector; the advowson was transferred to the Ecclesiastical Commissioners, the present Rectory was built in Coleshill Street, and Rectory Park was transferred by the Canon to the local community.

The prehistoric and Roman periods in the Sutton Coldfield area

Michael Hodder

INTRODUCTION

Recent research has considerably increased our knowledge of the prehistoric and Roman periods in the area around Sutton Coldfield. This article reviews the evidence now available and the methods used to obtain it.

DEFINITION OF AREA (see map)

The area considered in this article is the physical region which formed the medieval Sutton Chase; it is bounded on the south and east by the River Tame, on the north by the Bourne Brook, and on the west by Barr Beacon. The river and stream valleys are occupied by floodplains and gravel terraces. The eastern part of the area is on Keuper Marl, a clayey formation, with extensive covers of sandy glacial drift, which together result in medium to good quality agricultural land. The centre and north are on Keuper Sandstone and are generally good quality land. The higher land to the west, rising to Barr Beacon, has sandy pebbly soils developed on Bunter Pebble Beds and Hopwas Breccia. It has little surface water and its soils are prone to drought and to the removal of nutrients by leaching, thus it is poorer agricultural land than the rest of the area; indeed, it was heathland until the early 19th century when it was enclosed and brought into cultivation.

The west and south of the area are now predominantly built-up and the north, east and extreme west are predominantly open land used for agriculture and recreation.

SOURCES OF EVIDENCE

The evidence consists of objects of stone, metal and pottery, found by chance, through fieldwalking, or in excavation, and structures surviving as earthworks, visible as cropmarks or located in excavation. Chance finds of objects have been made mainly by gardening in built-up areas and from worn surfaces in recreational areas where there is public access. The objects found by chance tend to be the larger and more distinctively shaped stone objects, and distinctive metal objects, particularly coins. Pottery, even if it is seen, is unlikely to be recognised as significant by the layman and therefore not retrieved. Often the exact location of a chance find is not known. Where the object is now lost and known only through a written description both the place in which it was found and the form of the object may be in doubt.Even if the location is known, objects may have arrived there in material brought from elsewhere, for example in topsoil for a garden. Despite these difficulties, chance finds are the only type of evidence available from the built-up parts of the Sutton Coldfield area.

Fieldwalking involves walking up and down a ploughed field picking up objects from the surface; this method is therefore confined to existing arable land. The quantity and type of material observed and picked up in fieldwalking depends on lighting conditions, the state of weathering of the soil, and soil colour and dampness. The material found normally consists of stone objects and pottery. Fieldwalking in the Sutton Coldfield area was undertaken by the writer in 1980 and 1981 as part of a study of the development of 18th century common land, medieval parks, hamlets, medieval moated sites and isolated farmsteads. Sites for fieldwalking were therefore selected in relation to the medieval and post-medieval landscape rather than that of prehistoric and Roman times, but the sites were nonetheless widely distributed over the present arable land.

Earthworks of prehistoric and Roman date survive only in the west of the area, in places where they have not been levelled by building or ploughing. On arable land flattened earthworks may still be visible from the air as crop marks because of differences in the depth and moisture content of soil filling ditches and other features which result in variable rates of crop growth. There are, however, few crop marks in the Sutton Coldfield area, partly because there has been little aerial reconnaisance for archaeological purposes, and partly because much of the present arable land is on clay soils which do not normally produce crop marks. Most of the known crop marks have been recorded on the better drained soils of the gravel terraces in the river and stream valleys. Archaeological excavations have been undertaken at only four sites of prehistoric and Roman date in the Sutton Coldfield area: the burnt mounds and Roman road in Sutton Park, Loaches Banks, and the Sherifoot Lane Roman pottery kiln.

Members of the Local History Research Group fieldwalking at Middleton North Wood in 1980, with the help of a tape measure to ensure complete coverage.

LATE MESOLITHIC, ABOUT 6000-4000 BC

In this period agriculture was unknown, and food was obtained by hunting and gathering. The evidence for this period in the Sutton Coldfield area consists of flint tools and the cores, blades and waste flakes which are the debris from tool manufacture. Nearly all of the flintwork was found in fieldwalking. At some sites there are flint cores from which flakes were struck, and waste flakes but relatively few finished tools. This indicates a site where tool manufacture took place and was therefore some sort of settlement, even if it was only a temporary base-camp for hunting. Sites of this type, such as Manorial Wood and Wishaw Hall farm, tend to be near streams, which would provide drinking water and would also be clearings in a largely wooded landscape where trees would bear fruit. Other sites produce only a few flints, including finished tools and waste flakes but no cores; these are likely to be the result of tool loss and tool maintenance during hunting expeditions away from the base camp. Around Barr Beacon, for example, extensive fieldwalking produced only one finished tool and two waste flakes.

Sutton Chase showing the places referred to in the text

NEOLITHIC AND EARLY BRONZE AGE, ABOUT 4000-1500 BC

This period is distinguished from the Mesolithic by the introduction of agriculture and the use of different types of flint tools, tools of other stones, pottery and eventually metal. Several polished axes of flint and other stones have been found in the Sutton Coldfield area. These were probably used to clear the land of trees for agriculture. Other objects from this period are flint arrowheads and a bronze axe. There are possible round barrows, burial

Archaeological excavation in Mill Street, February 1989. Only two weeks of archaeological investigation were possible at this site, so the investigation was limited to a few exploratory trenches; although some post-holes were located, they appeared to be later than the Roman period. Other evidence — of the footings of earlier buildings, terracing of the steep hillside, and fragments of pottery, etc. — was from a later period. The preliminary report of the survey is in the Sutton Coldfield Local History Library. If another central Sutton site becomes vacant, it is to be hoped that a full archaeological survey can be made before it is redeveloped.

mounds of early Bronze Age date, at Kingstanding, Round Hill and Sutton Park. All three are in the west of the area; others may well have existed elsewhere but have been destroyed by agriculture or building.

MIDDLE BRONZE AGE, ABOUT 1500-1000 BC

The evidence for this period in the Sutton Coldfield area consists of two bronze palstaves and several 'burnt mounds'. The palstaves or small axes, are chance finds from Middleton and Curdworth. 'Burnt Mounds' are mounds of heat-cracked pebbles and charcoal about 15m across, usually adjacent to streams. Several of these sites have been found in the

Birmingham area and some of them have been dated by the radiocarbon method to the period 1500-1000 BC. A burnt mound near Middleton Hall was recorded in 1913 but was destroyed in the 1930's and a group of six mounds in Sutton Park was discovered and partly excavated in 1926. More burnt mounds have been identified in the Sutton Coldfield area by recent fieldwork and research. At Middleton New Park a mound has been found, while concentrations of heat-cracked pebbles on field surfaces at Wishaw Hall Farm and at Alder Wood in Drayton Bassett are probably burnt mounds. Several large mounds near the Chester Road at Berwood were removed in the 19th century and were said to have been composed of broken stones; these may well have been burnt mounds.

Burnt mounds have been thought to be the remains of cooking areas, but where they have ben excavated they have not produced any animal bones or pottery that might be expected if this were the case. It has also been suggested that they are the debris from sauna baths in which steam was produced by pouring water onto heated stones; this practice is known among North American Indians. Whatever their true interpretation, the mounds are evidence for the existence of settlements which must have accompanied them.

IRON AGE, ABOUT 500 BC—Ad 43

There is no evidence for the late Bronze Age (about 1000 - 500 BC) in the Sutton Coldfield area. The only object which is definitely of Iron Age date is a torc or neck ornament found near Middleton Hall. The other objects and structures described here are not securely dated to the Iron Age but are likely to be so by comparison with similar evidence from other areas. The site once known as Loaches Banks, adjacent to the Bourne Brook, survived as an earthwork until the late 18th century but was subsequently levelled by ploughing and is now only visible as a crop mark. An 18th century drawing, excavations in 1959, and recent aerial photographs show that the site consisted of a subrectangular area of about 100m long and 60m wide enclosed by three slight banks and ditches; the interior of the enclosure was occupied by slight scoops and gullies which may have been the remains of huts. No dating evidence was obtained from Loaches Banks, but similar sites elsewhere have been dated to the Iron Age. At Alder Wood, crop marks show three sides of a ditched rectangular enclosure measuring about 25m by 20m with faint traces of internal features. This site is comparable to farmstead enclosures of Iron Age and Roman date in the Tame Valley north of Tamworth. Crop marks of possible field enclosures are visible near Middleton Hall, on Bodymoor Heath, and near Hill Farm Cottages; the

Iron Age sites in the Tame valley were similarly surrounded by ditched field enclosures.

Fieldwalking near the Alder Wood site produced two sherds of probably Iron Age pottery; these are likely to indicate the site of a settlement because Iron Age pottery is not very hard-fired and is therefore unlikely to survive for long on field surfaces, so if it is found by fieldwalking it has probably come from settlement remains recently disturbed by ploughing.

ROMAN, AD 43-400

The field enclosures described above are as likely to be Roman as Iron Age in date. The only structures in the Sutton Coldfield area which are definitely of Roman date are the Roman road known as the Ryknild Street, part of which is well preserved in Sutton Park and the pottery kiln discovered recently at Sherifoot Lane, Four Oaks. The Roman Road was probably constructed during the campaigns of Ostorius Scapula about AD47 as a military line of communication between forts at Wall, near Lichfield, and Metchley, near Birmingham University. It consists of a central bank of gravel 9m wide between two discontinuous flanking ditches 19m apart. The ditches were probably dug as initial laying-out lines rather than as quarries; gravel for the road was obtained from shallow scoops beyond the ditches.

The Sherifoot Lane pottery kiln was discovered during the construction of a garden pond in 1987. Subsequent excavation showed that its main products were jars and bowls, datable to no earlier than the late 2nd century A.D. The presence of the kiln does not necessarily imply settlement; it is more likely to have been a rural industry.

The objects dateable to the Roman period consist of a carved stone, coins and more pottery. The stone and the coins were chance finds, mainly in gardening, and the pottery is from fieldwalking. The stone, found in Thornhill Park, is a sandstone block carved into a head. It is a type of carving common in northern Britain and may have been brought from there in recent times. A hoard of coins found in a pottery vessel at Wiggins Hill in the 19th century is likely to have been hidden near a settlement. A number of single coins are chance finds from the western part of the area, which is now built-up. Some of these may, like the carved stone, have been brought to the area in recent times and subsequently lost or discarded.

The distribution of Roman pottery found by fieldwalking is likely to provide a more accurate picture of the extent of settlement and agriculture in the Roman period than chance finds of coins. Roman pottery has been found in several places in the eastern and northern parts of the area, but not

1. The Sherifoot Lane
Roman Pottery Kiln.
General View (above),
showing the stokehole in
the foreground and the flue
and firing chamber beyond.

2. The Sherifoot Lane
Roman Pottery Kiln.
Detail of the firing
chamber (right), showing
the pedestals which
supported a clay floor
on which the pots were
stacked. Scale rods are one
metre long, in both
photographs.
                Photographs by
                    Paul Booth,
        Warwickshire County
                        Museum

in the present arable land in the extreme west. Since pottery was plentiful in the Roman period and is well made, it survives for long periods on the surface of a ploughed field. A few sherds of Roman pottery are therefore unlikely to indicate the site of a settlement but are probably the result of manuring and hence are evidence for Roman arable land. Broken pottery was thrown, together with domestic refuse, onto a dungheap adjacent to a farmstead and was incorporated into the ploughsoil when the dungheap was spread over the field as manure. The presence of small quantities of Roman pottery at several sites therefore indicates the extent of exploitation in the Roman period of what is now the main agricultural part of the Sutton Coldfield area. The only site that is likely to have been a settlement is near Shenstone Park Farm, where fieldwalking produced large unweathered sherds with fresh breaks. The absence of Roman pottery from the west of the area, despite extensive fieldwalking here, suggests that this part of the area was used as rough pasture. A trench dug through the Roman road in Sutton Park in 1936 revealed that the soil below it is a podzol, a soil in which all nutrients have been lost by leaching, which would have formed under heathland vegetation. In addition, no cropmarks of field systems are visible in the present arable land of the extreme west, even though the sandy, pebbly soils here are particularly suitable for cropmark production.

THE ROMAN AND LATER LANDSCAPES

It was noted above that sites for fieldwalking were selected in relation to the medieval and post-medieval landscape. Sufficient sites produced Roman pottery to enable comparisons to be made between land use and settlement patterns in the area in the Roman period and those of later periods. The broad pattern is identical; the eastern and northern parts were most exploited because it had the best agricultural land, while the west was not intensively exploited because of its poorer soils. The details of settlement appear to differ. Shenstone Park Farm is the only site at which there was both Roman and medieval occupation, and even here the medieval site, which is moated, has usually been considered to have been a hunting lodge since it is situated within Shenstone Park, a medieval deer park. Roman pottery has also been found in the area of the medieval deer park around Middleton Hall. These occurrences suggest a change in land-use from the Roman to the medieval periods; when these parks were created in the early 13th century they are likely to have been rough pasture rather than arable land. Similarly the quantity of Roman pottery found at medieval settlement sites is not sufficient to suggest that there were Roman settlements on these sites, but it is more likely to be the result of manuring arable land with domestic debris. The manuring activity does however imply associated settlements and there is no reason to suppose that the number of settlements in the Roman period was significantly less than in the Middle Ages. From this it can be inferred that there was widespread abandonment of settlement at the end of the Roman period. Subsequent medieval settlements cultivated the same land, but did not occupy the same sites as, the Roman settlements.

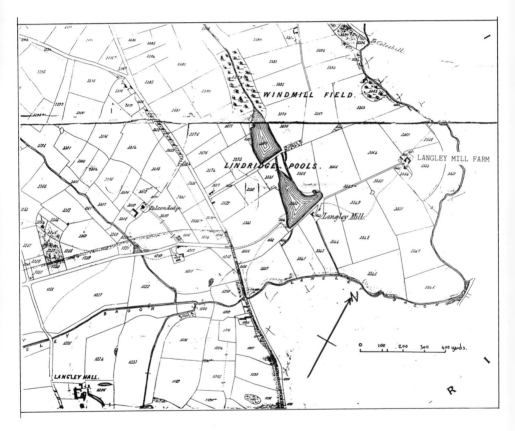

Valuation Survey, 1856, showing the location of Langley Mill

Langley Water Mill

by Ken Williams

LANGLEY WATER CORN MILL stood in a field off the Lindridge Road, below the dam of Langley Pool. It has the distinction of being one of two Sutton mills that were not worked by the water rising in Sutton Park. Langley water mill and Hill Hook Mill both had their own independent water supply.

The owners of the mill lived at Langley Hall, which was occupied in 1298 by the De Bereford family. We have no exact date for when the first pool was created or the mill built, the earliest reference being in the year 1604, when Langley Mill Pool was granted in perpetuity to Edward Pudsey of Langley Hall. This grant was made by the Warden and Society of Sutton Coldfield, the then Warden being George Pudsey.

The lease stated that he was to pay to the Corporation rent of five shillings per annum. The pool was there described as being a mill pool, suggesting that the mill may have been already in existence.

The first name we have for a miller at the corn mill is Richard Bell. All we know of him is his will; on his death bed in 1670, not having made a will, he declared his intentions before witnesses, and this was duly accepted as a nuncupative will and probate granted: "the said testator beinge asked by Alise Collins if itt pleased God to dispose of him who he would give his estate unto, he answered I give it to Ann Brothers who should have it". There is no mention in the rather perfunctory inventory of anything connected with his trade (it was valued at £23-9-0), but he is there described as "late of Langley within the Parish of Sutton Coldfield in the County of Warwick, miller".

Henry Pudsey of Langley Hall died in 1678 and his property was divided, Langley descending to his younger daughter, Ann, who married William Jesson Esq. in 1696. In their Manors of Langley and Wishaw, the Jessons had:

20 messuages; 6 cottages; 26 gardens; 26 orchards; 1 Dove House;
1 windmill; 1 watermill; 500 acres of land; 140 acres of meadow;
250 acres of pasture; 10 acres of wood; 20 acres of furze and heath.

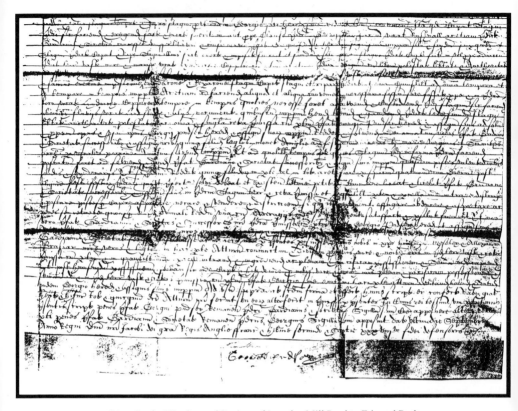

*Grant by the Warden and Society of Langley Mill Pool to Edward Pudsey,
this is the bottom half, with the signature of the Warden, George Pudsey.*

It is interesting to note that, included in the property, in addition to the watermill, which was Langley water corn mill, was a windmill. There had been a windmill at Langley in a field adjacent to the mill pool, which is shown on later maps as Windmill Field.

In order to increase the quantity of water for the mill, Jesson applied to the Corporation for a lease to build a second pool just upstream of the first pool, and the lease was duly granted:

"By indenture of lease bearing date 22nd October 1697, reciting that the Warden and Society had formerly granted liberty to Edward Pudsey to make a dam and pool in the waste ground in Sutton, called the Linderich near Langley Mills, for the use of the said mills, under the yearly rent of 5 shillings, and further reciting that the fishing

Lindridge Pool dam

Langley Mill Pool

Sluice gate at Langley Mill Pool

in the said pools was found to be prejudicial not only to the mills but the fish there, and after the fishing to supply the mills and preserve the fish; which inconveniences might be prevented by making another pool at the tail of the old pool, and thereupon William Jesson had made his request to the Warden and Society for a New grant to make a new dam and pool at the tail of the old one for the purpose aforesaid; It was witnessed that the Warden and Society granted the said William Jesson free liberty to make such a new dam and pool to contain in quantity as much ground as the said old pool then contained, and for that purpose to get turves and soil upon the waste ground called Lindridge, near and convenient to the same, and to fish the said new pool when made from time to time at his will and pleasure, to have and to hold such liberty to make the said new dam and pool when made for 1,000 years from the date thereof, at the yearly rent of 3 shillings, as also 6 bottles of wine and a dish of fish to the Warden then being, at all times during the term when it should be due at Michaelmas only''.

On the reverse of the lease it is explained that the wine and fish were to be paid only when the pool was fished by being drained down, a practice which explains why the mill had been short of water whenever such fishing had taken place. Langley water mill was the only Sutton mill to have two pools made for it.

A survey by John Snape of the Jesson lands made in 1776 shows the mill pool to be over 5 acres in extent; the dam has a road over it and a line of trees and bushes just below its slope. At the south-west corner of the pool an overflow is marked, whilst towards the other end of the dam is the sluice to control the flow of water to the mill. From the position of the tail-race it seems likely that the waterwheel was in the end of the mill building, protected from the elements. There is no pictorial or other evidence to verify its structure or layout, or the type of wheel installed. After working the mill machinery, the water followed a course through Mill Meadow and Low Pasture before emptying into Langley Brook.

The mill is mentioned in a letter of the Rector, R.B. Riland, to his wife, dated 11th August 1786 from Glasgow:

''P.S. Pray ask William Marigold whether the Langley Mill wants water and tell him he must not let the Bolt be in my abscence; let him grease the wheel of the new chair often''.

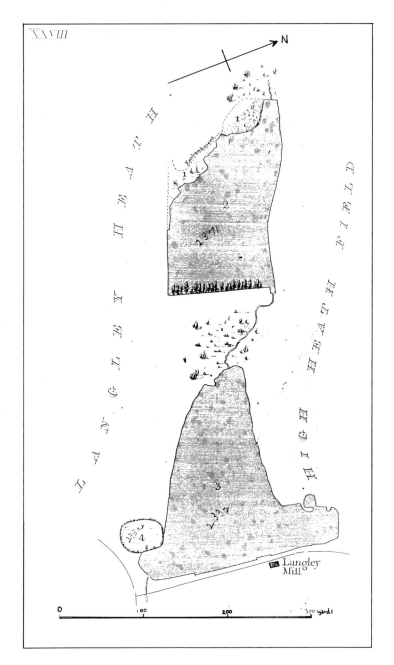

Corporation survey, c.1811

The bolt, or emptying of the pool, was clearly a great event in the neighbourhood, and may have been necessary to repair the dam if the mill was not getting its proper supply of water.

A survey of corporation property made 20 years later shows both pools, Lindridge Pool being 5 acres 2 roods 9 perches, Langley Mill Pool 5a.2r. 10p., their valuations being £8 and £15 respectively. Andrew Hackett of Moor Hall was the tenant of Lindridge Pool, and William Jesson still had Langley Mill Pool; although the mill is marked on the plan, the miller is not named.

The mill was up for sale in 1823, described as being the property of the late Mrs Elizabeth Pudsey Lynch, and including house, mill, premises, garden etc., A lease of 1835 to William Hind describes a

"farm with barns, stables and other outbuildings thereto belonging
called Langley Mill, Mill House, Mill Pool with all and singular and
going gear and machinery".

There were also 42 acres of land, and it was known as Starkey's Farm, the name of the farmer in the 1776 survey, also occurring in the 1830 directory as "Tim Starkey, miller at Langley". The mill is shown on the 1857 parish Valuation map, when John Bennell was the miller, possibly one of the last to work it, as by 1888 it had disappeared, having served the area for over 250 years.

Steam power superseded water power, and today the mill cannot be traced, although an archaeological investigation may prove fruitful. The site belongs to the water authority, and adjoins their sewage works. However, the pools remain to give sport to fishermen and pleasure to ramblers, and should be a lasting reminder of Langley Water Mill for generations to come.

———————

Wills and Inventories

by Gene Hetherington

WILLS AND INVENTORIES of former residents of Sutton Coldfield were studied for the period 1695-1710. The information to be gained from wills is usually as follows:

1. Name, occupation, and district or place of residence of the testator, e.g. Thomas Turner of "the fouer oakes", yeoman.

2. Details of the testator's family, names of widow and children, if any, number of children, and possibly details of more distant relatives, or friends and neighbours; e.g. John Cartwright the elder, cordwainer, mentions in his will his wife, Mary, and five sons, John, Symon, Thomas, William, and Joseph. His daughter, Margarett, is also remembered, and a request made regarding her welfare: "I desire her mother to bee kinde to her and to mainteyne her dureing her Life if she shall think well to continue and inhabite with her."
Edward Est, gentleman, bequeathes money to two sisters and to seven nephews and six nieces, all named in full.
John Vesey, yeoman, of Maney, mentions three "cozens" by name.
James Honeyborne, cordwainer, names Samuel Twamley, miller, his friend and neighbour, as executor of his will.

3. Description and location of land and property, possibly including field names. In the will of Thomas Addyes of Maney, gentleman, property is disposed of in Great Barr, Aston, Perry Barr, and Sutton Coldifeld, with details of field names and tenants, e.g. "all those meadows called Park Meadows and Blade Mill being and Lying in Sutton Park with all pooles, dams, streams and watercourses".

4. The literacy of testators and witnesses can be checked by noting whether they signed or put their marks to documents. There is an indication of the status of certain people in the community if their names appear a number of times as witnesses of wills, or as bondsmen when a person died intestate, or as appraisers of inventories; e.g. George Dodds was a witness six times in the wills studied, and an appraiser once; John Day, yeoman, was a bondsman or appraiser five times.

All the wills examined had inventories attached, as required by law at this period, so that probate could be granted. However of the 42 estates, there were only 27 wills, the remaining 15 people having died intestate. In these cases inventories were taken of all the deceased's property, and a bond entered into by relatives or friends, who agreed to administer the estate according to the law. Although legally subsidiary to the will, as a social document the inventory is more interesting; the contents of each room in the deceased's house are listed and valued, as are agricultural implements, crops, tools, and stocks of raw materials.

Information obtained from inventories is as follows:

1. The name, occupation, and place or district of residence of the deceased.

2. Money value of goods, remembering that wealth in property, land, or on loan as an investment is not included. John Addyes. Esquire, of Moorehall, was the wealthiest testator of those studied. Of the total inventory sum of £749-18-10, £300 is accounted for by "debts sperate and desperate" owed to him, an indication of considerable business activity; his household goods were worth £236-2-10, three times as much as those of the next wealthiest testator; e.g. in the "Dyneing Roome", which was on the first floor, were "three Tables, one Skreen, one Dozen of Turkey worke Chairs halfe a Dozen of Leather Chairs, one looking Glass". The linen included forty pairs of sheets, and the plate was valued at £30.

3. By comparison, the great poverty of some of the people is clear from the inventories, e.g. that of William Nicklin, labourer, of Sutton Coldfield. The total value of his possessions was £4-9-6, the most valuable item being "one old Cow £1-6-8". His cooking utensils consisted of "one iron pott" and "one old brass Kettle". A value of 2/6 was put on his 'wareing apparrell and money in his pockett".

4. The size and layout of the houses can be estimated; Moor Hall is probably the most interesting. It includes:
Ground floor: "Hall House. Parlour. Kittchen. Brew house, washe house. darey. Pantery. passage to ye Kitchen. Buttery."
First floor: "Dyneing Roome over the Hall. ye Chamber over ye Buttery. Passage above Stairs. Chamber over ye parlour. Studdy. Chamber over the Kitchin. Chamber over the Brewhouse".
Second floor: "Chamber over the parlour Chamber. Chamber over the Buttery Chamber. Chamber over the Studdy. Chamber over the Dyning Room".

A 'joyned bedstead', showing the bed-curtains open, the featherbed or mattress, and the valence or fringe concealing the wooden framework

Moor Hall c.1800; possibly little changed since John Addys's day, but long since demolished and rebuilt

Location not stated: "Cheese Chamber. Malt Chamber".

Outbuildings: "New Barne. Old Barne. pigg stye. yard. Coach House Chamber. Stable".

5. Numbers and variety of beasts kept and quantity and types of crops grown.

Of forty inventories, twenty-nine listed cows, from 1 to 24 in number; Thomas Heath of Greaves owned 24.

Twenty-five listed sheep, from 6 to 300 in number; Thomas Addyes of Maney owned 300.

Fifteen listed pigs, from 1 to 6, and twenty-one listed horses, from 1 to seven. Only the larger farmers kept bulls, seven in all. Poultry and bees are not mentioned many times, but may have been omitted because their value was so low; e.g. Thomas Vesey, a considerable farmer, had stock worth £70-19-10, but geese and hens are valued at 10/- only.

Crops grown were rye, barley, pease, corn, oats and hay; Francis Cooke of Bulls Farm had "corn and grain and hay in ye Barn" to the value of £109-6-8; this would have been after the harvest, as he died in September.

Thomas Vesey of Maney, who died in May, had barley, oats, pease, and hard corn "upon ye ground" (i.e. growing in the fields) to the value of £40-11-4, but only corn to the value of £11-5-0 in "ye house and barne".

6. Value of tools and stocks of raw materials for a man's trade. In these inventories the value put on stocks and tools is surprisingly small; the only considerable sum listed is for Thomas Heath, carpenter, of Greaves:

"Boards, quarters etc. of Timber £50-00-0" and "Carpenters Twools etc £2-10-0". William Watton, blacksmith, left shop tools valued at £4-2-6 to his wife, Anne, desiring her at her death to leave to his son John "all and every my shop, tools, Bellows and implements of trade".

In the wills of the period, the emphasis placed on the portions or dowries of the daughters is very evident. As so many of the men died before their children were adult, sons who inherited estates were often made responsible for paying the portions to their sisters; thus John, son of John Addyes, is bequeathed the rents and profits of certain lands and properties on condition that he pays £1,000 to his sister Anne and £400 to his sister Elizabeth, if and when each attains the age of 21; another son, Thomas, is left property on condition that he pays £600 to bring Elizabeth's portion up

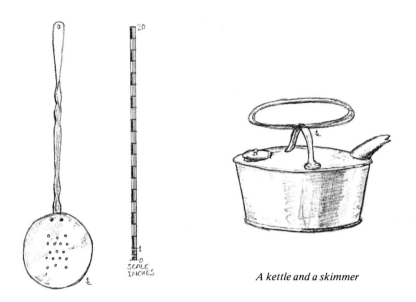

A kettle and a skimmer

to £1,000. An interesting item in this same will is the large sum of money, £40, left to the wife, Mary, to buy mourning for herself and her three youngest children.

Adequate provision appears to be made as a rule for the widow of the testator — her home and household goods left to her for life or until remarriage. Edward Peate of Hill allows that his widow, Margrett, may not wish to remain in the family home with her son Thomas (and presumably his wife); in which case, in addition to her legacy of two feather beds, half

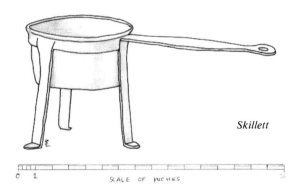

Skillett

of the household goods and £3 per year, Thomas is to give her "one hundred of cheese" and "ten strike" or bushels of corn and "yearly and every year one flitch of bacon."

The wealth in property and land of a testator cannot always be estimated, as it may be included in the residue left to the main heir. Thomas Addyes is the only one to have extensive property, but many of the more prosperous men owned at least one tenanted house in addition to their own homes. Thus Adrian Cockersall owned a house in Sutton and one at "Clif in Kingsbury" tenanted by John Willits. The will of Thomas Turner of Four Oaks lists his cottage and lands and a croft of two and a half acres. The complicated nature of some of the land-holdings is shown: "my part or portion of one running peece of meadow ground being the fourth part of three peeces of meadow ground lyeing together being occupied and used formerly between Thomas Orton and George Reppington". The use of common ground for arable farming is evident from the will of Margaret Wright of Holley Lane who leaves to her daughter, Martha, "all my corn or other grain in ye Barnes and also upon ye Comon ground".

Legacies of individual items of household goods, or even articles of clothing are common. John Taylour's daughter, Mary, inherited £20 and various items including "one joyned bedsted one fether bed one boulster and pillow two blankets one coverled with curtens and vallents and all belonging to it which stand in the parler", and also "one great Cetell (kettle) one midelling Cetell and one Litell Cetell". Edward Est, gentleman, left to the parish of Yardley one large book in folio called Fox's Acts and Monuments of the Christian Martyrs, and requested that he be buried in the family burial place at Yardley. Thomas Addyes asked that he be "decently buried in the parish church of Sutton Coldfield in the Warden's Chancel". The only charitable bequests are by John Addyes, £5, and John Turner of Hill, £2, for the poor of Sutton Coldfield.

Two complete inventories follow this article: the first, of Adrian Cockersall, includes a considerable value of household goods, £65-2-0 out of a total of £151-8-0, and is of particular interest because of the meticulous detail in the listing of the contents of the house; the inventory of Eliza Naylor is more of an amusing curiosity, as almost her only possessions were clothes. The reason for this becomes apparent on examining the burials section of the parish register: "Elizabeth Naylor being a servant maid that died at the Esquire Addyes of Moore Hall".

An analysis of the wills and inventories studied gives some idea of where the wealth of the inhabitants lay. As one might expect on seeing that

Eliza Naylor's inventory

"yeoman" is the most common description, the value of household goods is almost invariably exceeded by the value of agricultural goods, i.e. cattle, crops, and implements of husbandry. Even where a man had a trade, his agricultural interests seem to be as important; Thomas Heath, carpenter, had cattle, crops, etc. worth £190 and tools of his trade valued at only £2-10-0. On a smaller scale, Thomas Reeve, cooper, had two thirds of the value of his inventory in agricultural goods, £12-6-0, and tools valued at £1-6-8 only. In no case is there any evidence that a tradesman was engaged in any business outside the locality, and there are no debts owed to suppliers of raw materials or debts owed by customers as one finds in the inventories of the smiths and tanners of Birmingham. Agriculture is predominant; where an inventory shows little value in agricultural goods it is usually possible to find a reason. John Perkins described himself as "sick and weake of body" when he made his will in 1698, and did not appear to have any possessions or home of his own when he died in 1703; Ralph Norris with only 18/- listed for seven sheep and eight fleeces is described in the burials register as aged 73 and blind.

A study of household goods in the inventories shows that furnishings were adequate but unsophisticated. Books are very seldom mentioned, John Turner's being valued at 16/-; Thomas Addyes had pictures in the parlour. Only a few houses had a looking glass and there is very little silver or plate listed. However, the analysis shows that houses in the district were of a reasonable size, six or seven rooms in all on two floors was usual; many houses had three floors with large garrets or cocklofts, only a few had cellars.

Sizes of families can be estimated by the numbers of children mentioned in wills. There are surprisingly few large families, and those mostly among the more prosperous inhabitants — possibly their children were better fed and nurtured and stood a better chance of survival. John Agott, husbandman, left what little property he had to his wife, with small legacies to kinsmen; according to the parish register, two of his children died in August 1672 and three in September 1681. Some of the older testators would have outlived their children, e.g. James Honeyborne, who died in 1707 is described in the register as "old James Honeyborne", two of his sons having died in 1698 and 1699, but a daughter was still living when he made his will; it is interesting that he had little opinion of his son-in-law, and left his property in trust for the benefit of his daughter, Mary Greene, "without any account thereof to her husband notwithstanding her marriage".

An Inventory of the Goods and Chattles of Eliza Nealor of the Parish of Sutton in the County of Warwick A.D. 1703

	£ - s - d
In money in her purse	02-08-0
Small Linnen	01-00-0
for Showes and Stockins	00-05-0
for her Shifts	00-12-0
for Pette coats	01-02-0
for Manteys	01-10-0
for her Stayes	00-16-0
for one pair of Sheets & 20 pound of Flax	00-15-0

Apprized by Eliza, the wife of Jn. Taylor and Widd. Tunke of the parish of Sutton Coldfield.

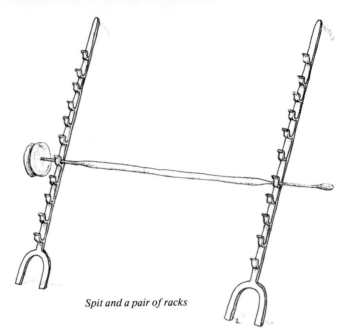

Spit and a pair of racks

A true Inventory of the Goods and Chattels of Adrian Cockersall of Sutton Coldfield in Com. War. yeoman Lately deceased praised the 26th day of Aprill 1707 by us whose names are under written.

	£ - s - d
Imprimis his wareing Apparrell & Mony in his purs	10-00-00
Item in the Kitchen 2 brass panns 4 brass Potts 9 Kettles) 2 brass skellits one warmeing pan 4 brass Candlesticks) 1 Coper Can & 1 Scimer att)	04-00-00
2 Iron driping pans 3 Spitts 1 pare of Racks 1 Jack) 1 Cliver one Choping knife 2 Smoothing Irons 4 Iron) Candle Sticks 1 ffrying pan 2 ffurmes 2 dressers a Table) a Bacon Cratch 4 Cheares 1 Gun & 3 dozen of Trenchers at)	03-03-00
one harth Grate in ye same roome 1 ffire Grate one pare of) Tongs one Iron ffire Shovel & 2 pare of Pott Geales all at)	01-00-00
4 fflitches of Bacon att	02-00-00
21 Pewter disshes 3 dozen & a half of plates 4 porengers) 2 salts 3 tundisshes 2 pewter Guns 4 pewter Cans 2 quarts) 1 half pint & a pint 2 pewter Chamber potts a Caudle Cup) a peuter bason & 3 dozen of spoons all att)	06-09-00
Item in the Parlor one Clock and Case	02-10-00
one ffether bead and all there to belonging at	03-00-00

	£ - s. - d.
1 Large Table 1 litle Table 3 ffurmes 6 fflagg Cheares all att	01-05-00
Item in the buttery 1 Joyned Cubard, Cheise press 1 Lether) bottle 1 Churn 1 wooden bottle 6 Chesfords 2 shooters) 1 Little Cubard all at)	01-10-00
Item in the sellar 5 barrells a Glass Case & 1 long Bench at	01-10-00
Item in the brew house 2 small brass ffurninses 1) Kneading Trough & Cover 2 Tubs 5 peals 5 Kimnells one) Thrall one Strike Eight Baggs & 2 Sives all att)	05-05-00
Item in the best Chamber 1 Joyned bead stid a ffether bead) & all belonging to it att)	03-00-00
i Hangin press 1 Chest 1 round Table 6 fflagg Cheares 2) Lether Chears 1 Chamber grate & a side board table all att)	02-10-00
Item in the Closit 2 Lether Trunks & 1 small Table att	00-12-00
Item in the Chamber over the parler 2 ffether beads &) half headed bead stids with all belonging to them att)	05-00-00
1 Cubard 1 Table & 2 Chears att	00-10-00
Item in the Chamber over ye butery 2 flock beads & bead) stids & all belonging to them 2 Cofers 2 boxes & a Trunk) one Joyned Chear & a looking Glass all att)	03-05-00
Item in the Two Cocklofts 1 ffether bead & bolster & bead) stid and all belonging to it att)	02-10-00

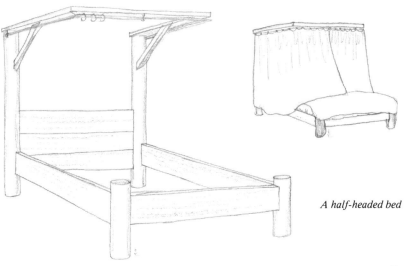

A half-headed bed

Glossary of Terms used in the Inventory

Bakon cratch	Rack to hang sides of bacon on, near the ceiling
Caudle cup	Cup for warm drinks
Chaff bed	Mattress stuffed with straw or chaff
Chesford	Cheese vat
Close flaskett	Basket with a lid
Diaper	A napkin or towel
Flagg cheares	Chairs with seats of woven reeds
Furme, form	Bench
Gears	Harness
Hangin press	A large cupboard for clothes
Hempen	A rough cloth made of hemp
Holand	Fine linen
Hookes	Curved tools with a cutting edge
Huckaback	Strong linen with a rough surface
Hurden	Coarse fabric
Jack	Device for turning a spit
Joyned (furniture)	Made by a joiner
Kimnell	Wooden tub
Muncorn	Mixture of wheat and rye sown and grown together
Pot geales	Swinging crane over a kitchen grate
Racks	Iron bars for holding a spit
Shooter	Board placed between cheeses under a press
Stall (of bees)	Hive
Strike	A measure equivalent to a bushel
Thrall	A stand for barrels
Trencher	Wooden plate
Tumbril	A tipping cart
Tundish	Funnel

	£ - s. - d.
one Chaff bead & bead stid and all belonging to it att	01-00-00
1 Wagon Rope 4 strikes a Muncorn 1 Coffer 1 Close) fflaskett 1 Table & Joyned ffurm att)	02-00-00
1 Holand sheet 3 pare of fflaxen sheets 6 pare of Hempen) sheets 5 pare of Hurden Sheets 2 Hucabac Table Clothes) 2 dozen of Napkins of ye same. 6 fflaxen Napkins 6) Diaper Napkins 2 Holland Pillobears 2 flaxen ones & 1) of Hempen 2 Holand Sideboard Table Clothes & 12 Corse) Towells all at)	13-03-00
ffour Swine	att 03-10-00
a wagon at £6 a Tumbril at £3 both	att 09-00-00

	£ - s. - d.
1 plow 2 Harows & a wheel barrow	att 00-16-00
1 Tub in the barn	1-00-00
Gears in the Stable for 5 horses	00-15-00
2 Spades 2 Axes 6 fforkes 2 Riding Hookes 1 back hooke	
4 Reaping hooks & all ye other implements in husbandry	att 01-00-00
1 Manger & Cratch	02-00-00
4 Cows & 3 Heafers	att 14-00-00
2 Mares & 3 horses	att 14-00-00
fflax in the Ruff & a Stone Maltt Mill att	01-10-00
19 yew sheep & lams & 29 baron sheep	att 06-10-00
a Remainder of a hay rick	att 02-10-00
6 Stalls of Bees	att 01-10-00
1 buckit & Chain	att 00-05-00
winter corn upon the ground	att 05-00-00
oates upon the ground	att 04-10-00
Barly upon the ground	06-00-00
Pease upon the ground	att 01-10-00
all other things ffergott & old Lumber	01-00-00
The total sum of this Inventory is	151-08-00

praised by us the day & year within written

William Lunn
Hen. Sedgwick

Probate May 1707.

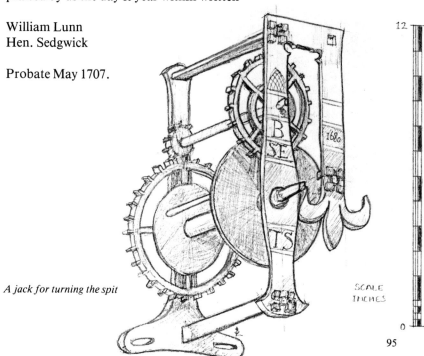

A jack for turning the spit

SCALE
INCHES

95

Analysis of Wills and Inventories for Sutton Coldfield, 1700-1710

	Name	Date	Will or Inventory	Occupation or status	Place of Residence	Total value of inventory £ s d	Household Goods £ s d	Agricultural Goods £ s d	Miscellaneous £ s d	Rooms/floors in the house	No. of children mentioned
1.	John Addyes	1706	W & I	Esquire	Moore Hall	789-18-10	236-02-10	232-16-00	321-00-00 (£300 debts)	20/3	5
2.	Thomas Addyes	1700	W & I	Gentleman	Maney	312-01-08	58-00-00	194-00-00	60-06-08 (£40 debts)	9/2	6
3.	John Agott	1701	W & I	Husbandman	Sutton Coldfield	27-19-00	4-15-00	21-14-00	1-10-00	5/2	0
4.	George Bentley	1708	W only	Tallow Chandler	Sutton	—	—	—	—	—	3
5.	John Bickley	1706	I only	Miller	Hill	19-03-04	3-12-10	13-15-00	1-15-06 (10/6 for tools in mill)	6/2	no will
6.	John Cartwright the elder	1707/8	W & I	Cordwainer	Sutton Coldfield	63-03-01	37-01-09	18-08-00	7-13-04 (leather £6)	12/3	6
7.	Adrian Cockersall	1707	W & I	Yeoman	Sutton Coldfield	151-08-00	65-02-00	75-06-00	11-00-00	11/3	3
8.	Francis Cooke	1700	I only	Yeoman	Bulls Farm	334-05-08	88-14-00	205-01-08	40-00-00 (£20 debts)	9/3	no will
9.	John Cooper	1710	I only	Naylor	Sutton Coldfield	19-09-03	7-15-01	10-11-08	1-02-06	5	no will
10.	William Cooper	1710	W & I	Naylor	Sutton Coldfield	40-01-09	9-08-05	29-10-00	1-03-04	no details	2
11.	Thomas Cowper	1702	I only	Yeoman	Sutton Coldfield	17-19-06	2-14-00	14-01-00	1-04-06	probably 2	no will
12.	Edward Ensor the Younger	1707	I only	not given	Hill Hook	12-00-00	3-10-00	7-15-00	0-15-00	4	no will
13.	Edward Est	1703	W & I	Gentleman	Sutton Coldfield	4-04-00	2-16-00	—	1-08-00	1	0
14.	Edward Hargrave	1701	W & I	Husbandman	Langley Heath	79-19-09	18-05-10	57-15-07	3-18-04	7/2	0
15.	Benjamin Harris	1707	I only	Nailer	Hill Hook	24-05-06	6-09-06	16-08-04	1-07-08 (tools 6/8)	5 & shop	no will
16.	Thomas Heath	1710	W & I	Carpenter	Greaves	09-13-04	57-00-08	190-16-00	61-16-08 (Timber £50, tools £2-10-00)	9/2	0
17.	James Honeyborne	1707	W & I	Cordwainer	Sutton Coldfield	12-13-04	6-07-01	2-10-00	3-15-08 (tools 13/-)	4 & shop	1
18.	John James	1708	W & I	not given	Sutton Coldfield	19-19-00	18-04-00	1-15-00	—	7/2	several
19.	Elianor Kendrick	1704	W only	Single woman	Sutton Coldfield	—	—	—	—	—	0
20.	William Lines	1707	I only	Labourer	Maney	19-08-00	5-15-08	12-14-00	0-18-04	5	no will

No.	Name	Year	Type	Occupation	Place						
21.	Thomas Miles	1704	I only	not given	Sutton Coldfield	19-01-08	16-18-02	0-12-00	1-12-00	7/2	1
22.	Eliza Nealor	1703	I only	not given	Sutton Coldfield	8-08-00	0-15-00	—	7-13-00	—	—
23.	William Nicklin	1703	I only	Labourer	Sutton Coldfield	4-09-06	2-05-00	2-00-00	0-04-06	no details	no will
24.	Ralph Norris	1704	W & I	Labourer	Hill	17-07-00	0-14-00	0-18-00	15-15-00 (Notes, bills, & money)	no details	0
25.	Edward Peate	1710	W & I	Yeoman	Little Sutton	124-17-06	23-19-02	95-15-00	5-03-04	4/2	1
26.	John Perkins	1703	W & I	Husbandman	Sutton Coldfield	7-00-00	—	—	7-00-00	apparently	0
27.	Katherine Pickerill	1709	W & I	widow	Sutton Coldfield	6-03-06	4-03-00	—	2-00-06 (Money, Apparel, bond) No home	no details	0
28.	Joseph Raynor	1703	I only	not given	Sutton Coldfield	195-00-08	34-01-08	153-06-06	7-12-06	11/3	3
29.	Thomas Reeve	1710	I only	Cooper	Sutton Coldfield	18-17-02	3-19-06	12-06-00	2-11-08 (tools £1-06-08)	5 & shop	no will
30.	Richard Smith	1709	W & I	Yeoman or baker	Little Sutton	98-08-06	47-02-02	48-13-00	2-13-04	8/2	9
31.	William Spooner	1701	I only	not given	Sutton Coldfield	4-17-00	4-03-00	—	0-14-00	1	1
32.	William Taylor	1707	W & I	Yeoman	Sutton Coldfield	26-04-02	11-11-08	13-06-08	1-05-10	6/2	1
33.	Ann Taylor	1701	W & I	widow	Sutton Coldfield	23-19-06	6-11-06	16-05-00	1-03-00	3	3
34.	John Taylour	1701	W & I	Nailer	Little Sutton	12-03-00	4-18-00	5-16-00	1-09-00 (tools 5/-)	4 & shop	2
35.	John Turner	1704	W & I	Yeoman	Hill	30-14-00	15-13-06	3-15-00	15-09-06 (books 16/-)	4	0
36.	Sarah Turner	1700	I only	Widow	Sutton Coldfield	13-07-01	5-17-04	7-09-01	0-00-08	4/2	1
37.	Thomas Turner	1700	W & I	Yeoman	Four Oaks	34-16-07	7-09-00	3-01-07	not listed	0	1
38.	John Veysey	1708	W & I	Yeoman	Maney	26-17-00	20-17-00	6-00-00	6-00-00	6/3	0
39.	Thomas Vesey	1703	I only	not given	Maney	198-00-00	44-17-10	146-15-06	6-06-08	6/3	no will
40.	William Watton	1709	W & I	Blacksmith	Sutton Coldfield	51-18-04	24-05-10	16-00-00	11-02-06 (shop tools £4-02-06)	8/2	1
41.	Henry Wright	1704	W & I	Yeoman	Sutton Coldfield	71-06-10	16-17-04	47-07-00	7-02-06	not listed	2
42.	Margrett Wright	1708	W & I	Widow of Henry	Holley Lane	59-14-00	15-04-00	38-17-06	5-12-06	not listed	2

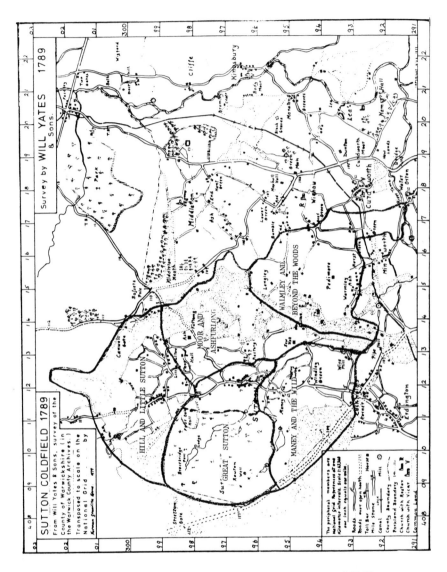

Approximate boundaries of the five 'quarters' of Sutton Coldfield

A Healthy Town? —
Observations on Burials, 1650-1727

By Honor and Clifford Parsons

POPULATION FIGURES FOR ENGLAND AND WALES before 1800 were recently published, ending centuries of uncertainty when some very inaccurate guesses were being made. The Parish Registers for over 400 parishes were analysed using sophisticated statistical methods and computer technology over a period of years by the Cambridge Group for the History of Population and Social Structure, culminating in the publication in 1981 of *The Population History of England, 1541-1871*, by E.A. Wrigley and R.S. Schofield. Their research revealed rapid growth in the first half of the 17th Century, slight decline in the second half, and a steady rise after 1700: 1600: 4,066, 132; 1650 : 5,220, 613; 1700 : 5,026, 877; 1750 : 5,739, 364. This decline in the second half of the century could be partly due to the facts that 1647,48 and 49 were famine years, that there were epidemics of smallpox at the end of the 17th and early in the 18th centuries, and that between 30% and 40% of children died before they were 14, largely from infection. The last major outbreak of plague, with 97,000 deaths, was in 1665, but other epidemic diseases with high rates of mortality were typhus, syphilis, tuberculosis, dysentery, and measles — this was often fatal to malnourished children. Summer diarrhoea, a form of dysentery affecting infants, and the cause of many deaths, occurred almost every year between mid-July and mid-September.

It should be possible to recognise deaths occurring as a result of an epidemic by reference to records of burials. These were kept in the parish church in three books — baptisms, marriages, and burials, — every event being recorded, usually just a name and a date, but sometimes place of abode or family relationships. With Sutton's population of about 1200, an average year would be one with 40 baptisms, 8 marriages, and 40 burials. If a severe illness occurred, causing a number of deaths in a short period, this would show up in the register as an unexpected clustering of events, and if the additional information as to family relationships or place of abode indicates the likelihood of contact between the victims, then an infection can be deduced.

But what constitutes an unexpectedly large number of burials? and how long is the short, well-defined period in which an epidemic would rage? and how is the context of the infection to be proved with so little background information? In an attempt to overcome these difficulties the accompanying tables have been constructed without thought of definition — they merely summarize all clusters of deaths in Sutton in the two periods 1650-74 and 1675-99.

Inspection of these tables shows no evidence of a devastating epidemic like plague, nor of seasonal outbreaks of severe summer diarrhoea; there is, however, a clear indication of a small epidemic confined to Hill in 1671. Of the 17 burials between March 15th and June 16th, at least 10, and possibly 12, were from Hill. The disease responsible cannot have been airborne (e.g. measles) or vector-borne (e.g. typhus), because the cases would not have been concentrated in such a relatively small area. The probability is that the disease was water-borne (e.g. dysentery), and originated from a contaminated water supply.

It was unusual for the Parish Clerk to record the place of residence in the register: on this occasion, he was perhaps impressed by the number of burials originating from Hill. Infections transmitted by contact are even more difficult to unravel; contact between individuals might be assumed if, for example, in any cluster or outbreak, several deaths occurred in two or more families. In fact, none of the clusters in the tables contains multiple deaths in more than one family, and usually only two members of that family are involved. Deaths of two children, or one parent and one child, need not necessarily be the result of transmitted infection, but when mother, father and child all die within a few days, (e.g. 7-17 September 1675), or when three or more children are involved, this is evidence for presuming an infectious origin. However, even this may not be conclusive: three Turnor children died in January 1643, on the 1st, 5th and 6th, but they are from three different Turnor families. Did the branches of the Turnor family have a family celebration and reunion at Christmas when all three were exposed to the same virulent infection? or were these deaths, all within a week, pure coincidence?

It is reasonable to assume that children are particularly susceptible to infectious diseases, and that many epidemics are virtually restricted to children. However, it is often impossible to be certain from the parish register how old children were when they died. For example, the children of John Agott:
Buried on 5.8.1672 child aged 4¾ years
15.8.1672 child aged 1¾ years

4.9.1681 child aged 8 ¼ years
8.9.1681 child aged ?
11.9.1681 child aged ?

It is apparently a convention that "children" are so called until they can be set to work, when they become 'son' or 'daughter', — but this does not solve the age question. It should be a simple matter to check age by looking back through the records of baptisms, but the repeated use of the same name (Mary dies; the next daughter is christened Mary), omissions, illegibility, gaps in the record, and migration in and out of the parish render this unreliable and often fruitless. The clerk often records the age of adults who die prematurely or who reach a ripe old age. The number of people living into their 70's, 80's, 90's — even over 100 (see 17.12.1663) suggests that longevity was commonplace in Sutton, at a time when the average life expectancy was 41 for males and 45 for females (these figures are for 1750-1850)

In some cases, especially accidents, the cause of death is given (e.g. mother and child dying within a few days as a result of childbirth), but usually no reason is given for the death. Henry Alsop was buried on July 3rd 1707, having been burnt to death in his house; his wife had been buried two months earlier, on May 9th; was Henry's death purely accidental, or perhaps a consequence of carelessness and apathy, — or did he commit suicide? Unfortunately the Coroner's papers for this period have not been preserved, so we are left guessing. On the other hand John Norris buried a wife and acquired a new one every few years (7 in all) — why did his wives fail to survive? When the wife and three children of John Bassit died over a period of two years, the possibility of tuberculosis must rank high, but other possible connections give no clue; for example, Christopher Braidhouse died while he was lodging with Widow Edly; Elizabeth Edly had been buried the previous week, on October 27th 1700; what connection was there, if any?

There were tragic causes of death, such as Widow Elinor Clibury and her son, drowned trying to recover a gosling from a marlpit (a pond formed where marl had been extracted) — the importance of the gosling to them, which cost them their lives, is a matter for conjecture. Jane Bayley, a servant of Mr Thomas Addyes of Maney, was buried in February 1668, having had her head cut off by William Addyes son of Thomas, who was alleged to be mentally defective. There is no record of what happened to William, as his name does not appear in the burial register for Sutton, but in 1670 Mr and Mrs Thomas Addyes died on the same day and were buried in a single grave (August 29th 1670); what had happened to them?

Deaths & Buryings.
Anno Dom: 1670.

There was Buryed the xxiijth of July Judeth } Corbett
Corbett widd late wife of Rowland Corbett of Asshington

There was buried the fifth Day of August a child of } Griffen
John Griffen's a boy named ffrancis

There was Buryed the viijth day of August Richard } Ashford
Ashford sen

There was Buryed the xviijth Day of August } Walker
David Walker

There was Buryed the xixth day of August } Hawkesford
Ann Hawkesford single woman named

There was Buryed the xxijth day of Augst the } Cartwright
wife of Symon Cartwright named Margaret

There was Buryed the xxiijth Day of August } Smith
John Smith of Peeway-box-lane

There was Buryed the same xxiijth of August Daniell Ashford

There was Buryed the same xxiijth Day of August } James
the Thomas James of Little Sutton

There was Buryed the xxvth Day of August the } Postoll
wife of Mr John Postoll named Elizabeth

There was Buryed the xxvjth Day of August the } Terryø
wife of william Terrye

There was Buryed the xxviijth Day of August } Tunkes
Richard Tunkes of Hannam Hyatt

There was Buryed the xxixth Day of August } Addyes
Mr Thomas Steges And Mrs Ann Addyes his } wife both in one grave

There was Buryed the first Day of September } Turnor
the wife of Thomas Turnor

There was Buryed the third day of September } Davies
Elizabeth Davies widd

There was Buryed the iiijth Day of September } Wright
william Wright of Little Sutton

There was Buryed the iiijth day of September } James
Thomas James of Little Sutton

There was Buryed the xth Day of September } Baylos
Mary Baylos of wormly single woman

There was Buryed the xxth day of September } Ashford
Thomas Ashford of

There was Buryed the 24th Day of
there was Buryed the

The Parish Register, burials

The register of burials is full of interest, but much more information is needed before it would be safe to draw conclusions of a kind which a modern medical officer would put in his report on mortality, such as causes of death, incidence of epidemics, and mortality rates in various age groups. However, the general impression is of a healthy, well-nourished and reasonably wealthy community with an expectation of life greater than the average for England and Wales as a whole.

Clusters of Burials, 1650-1674

Year	Between	Dates	Days	Deaths	Notes
1654	May 24	July 4	42	11	One period of 25 days with 8 deaths
1655	April 2	April 11	10	6	Child and wife of Mr J. Powell among the six
1657	Aug. 7	Sept. 21	46	16	Period of 20 days with 10 deaths Thomas Wooton and his wife
1658	Mar 31	April 18	19	6	Perhaps an epidemic
	May 12	May 27	16	7	with three waves causing 23 deaths
	June 10	June 28	19	10	Includes Thomas Fisher and his child
	Nov 4	Nov 19	16	7	
1659	Mar 2	Mar 31	30	10	
	Sept 2	Oct 25	54	12	Period of 27 days with 7 deaths
1660	Aug 29	Oct 6	39	12	
1664	Feb 1	Mar 6	35	9	
1668	Sept 17	Oct 19	33	10	Includes wife and child of William Wilkinson
1669	Feb 8	Mar 29	50	16	
	Oct 15	Nov 5	22	7	
1670	July 29	Sept 4	47	18	Perhaps a single epidemic
	Sept 15	Oct 21	39	12	with 30 deaths
	Nov 9	Nov 26	18	9	
1671	Mar 7	Apr 12	37	12	Between March 15th and June 16th 10 deaths occurred at Hill.

Year	Between	Dates	Days	Deaths	Notes
	May 1	June 23	55	9	Includes Mr Gawen Priest and child, two Cartwrights, Cowper and Rigg
1672	May 7	May 31	25	6	
1674	June 23	July 10	18	7	

Clusters of Burials, 1675-1699

Year	Between	Dates	Days	Deaths	Notes
1675	Jan 2	Feb 25	55	11	
	Aug 29	Sept 17	20	8	Includes William Burton his wife and his child
1676	Mar 10	Apr 25	47	12	Includes Isaac Whorwood and his child
1677	Jan 25	Mar 27	59	18	Includes two Jeffery alias Walkers
1678	Mar 31	May 2	33	10	
1680	Dec 21 1679	Jan 26	37	11	Includes Abell Cowper senior, Abell Cowper jr. and Richard Cowper - no clear evidence of all being in the same household. Also two Rastells, but may be separate households.
	Oct 12	Jan 4	84	23	Two Cowpers, perhaps unrelated. Wife and child of John Parker
1681	May 12	May 31	20	7	Two children of Thomas Wilcox
	Sept 4	Sept 22	19	8	Three children of John Agott
1684	Jan 12	Feb 19	39	16	Possibly two waves of an epidemic
	Mar 1	Mar 23	24	12	Includes wife and child of William Nicklyn
	July 29	Aug 31	34	11	Two Cowpers - from different districts
1685	Dec 15 1684	Jan 19	36	8	Includes wife and child of George Syar

Year	Between	Dates	Days	Deaths	Notes
	Mar 14	Apr 23	41	17	Includes Joseph Woodisson and wife
	June 14	June 30	17	6	Samuel Jeffery's wife and child
1688	Feb 27	Apr 25	58	12	
1689	May 5	May 27	23	7	
	June 20	July 30	41	9	Wife and child of John Saunders
	Oct 3	Dec 10	69	18	
1690	Mar 22	Apr 14	24	9	
	Dec 6	Dec 25	20	6	
1691	Apr 1	Apr 28	29	8	Two Turnors, probably unrelated
1695	Apr 6	May 1	26	7	
1698	July 27	Aug 23	28	8	

Pond at Bulls Lane; such ponds or 'marlpits', formed by the extraction of clay to be spread on the light soils of the fields of Sutton to improve fertility, were a common feature of the rural landscape. Coroner's papers survive for a few years in the 18th century, when drowning was the most frequent cause for an inquest; often the fatal scene was a marlpit, as it had been for Widow Clibury and her son 100 years before.

Trinity Hill, c.1800; the cottages in the foreground are on the site of the first Town School

The Origins of the Elementary School System in Sutton Coldfield

by Derek Redwood

INTRODUCTION

IN 1826 THE FIRST CHARITY SCHOOL to be built in the Royal Town of Sutton Coldfield opened its doors and admitted 39 boys. It heralded a new era in educational provision within the old borough. The school became known as the Town School and its opening brought to a conclusion the many years of bitterness and argument which preceded that event.

The purpose of this article is to tell the story behind that occasion, using the various sources to be found in the Local History Library in Sutton Coldfield.

ORIGINS

In 1528 Bishop Vesey, Sutton Coldfield's great benefactor, founded a Free School in Blind Lane (now Trinity Hill) to provide a classical education for the sons of the landed gentry who lived in or near the Royal Town. By 1727 the buildings and the school were said to be in a poor state of repair and the Master, Paul Lowe, reached an agreement with the Warden and Society to finance a new school room and house at a cost of £700. In return for the Corporation providing £400 towards that sum, Mr Lowe agreed that he and his successors would teach 12 boys of the town the skills of writing, arithmetic and English. The minutes of the Corporation dated 30th. November 1733 underlined their apparent determination to go further and to erect a school of their own —

> *"And it allfo agreed That the rent of the New Inclofure in Etchillhurft bottom Shall be likewife paid into the hands of the Church Wardens for the time being, for and towards the teaching or Endowment of a Scholl for Parifh Chilldren to learn Writing and Accounts as Abovesaid, or for other pious and secular ufes, for which purpofe A schoolmaster Shall be Elected by the Corporation At A Common Hall between Chriftmas and Candlemas Next. And Such Elections to be Continued yearly for ever."*

These good intentions do not seem to have been taken further for, on February 4th. 1734, it was decided to lease the School and adjoining Croft (in Blind Lane) to Mr Lowe. In return he agreed to instruct up to 12 boys, under fourteen years of age, in writing and Arithmetic. It was stipulated that

> *"Arithmatick . . . . Shall be taught as far as the four first rules . . . and it is further agreed that the present schoolmaster and his successors shall teach and Instruct . . . . in English a Class of the Parish Boys of Sutton."*

This would seem to be the first evidence of educational provision for the children of the ordinary parishioners and was separate from the Latin (or Grammar) School, run by Mr Lowe for those scholars whose parents could afford to pay for a classical education.

The next reference to schooling does not appear until 1778 when the Corporation agreed to pay a sum of £30 to the Reverend Richard Bisse Riland in order that he could obtain the services of a 'fit' person to instruct and teach the poor children of the Parish the skills of reading. In 1781 he

*Detail from Miss Bracken's prospect of Sutton (see page 6). In the foreground
is the Olde Pie Shoppe with its tall chimneys, partly obscuring some buildings
in Lower Parade; beyond them, the building with six windows, low-pitched roof,
pediment and belfry is the Town School of 1826. To the left, in Mill Street,
are the almshouses of similar style built under the same scheme (now a taxi-rank).
The workhouse is the tall building further up Mill Street; the cottages behind
survived until the end of the century. The Church is the dominant building,
its imposing character having been somewhat exaggerated by the artist.*

provided the Warden and Society with a brief report of his achievements. At a cost of £20 a total of 55 children had been taught reading, writing, arithmetic and knitting. It is not clear how the teaching was organised but there were only 6 children attending the school at the time of his summary. This would suggest, perhaps, that groups of children were taught on a part-time basis, fitting in with the needs of their parents, many of whom were employed in the seasonal demands involved in earning a living from the land. This then was the known extent of schooling in Sutton Coldfield prior to a series of events, which, commencing in the late 18th. century, were to culminate in the Scheme of 1826 — a plan designed to give a basic education to the children of the parish, regardless of parental income or aspiration.

ARGUMENTS

During the 18th. century, in particular, there had been growing unrest and dissatisfaction with the manner in which the Warden and Society administered the affairs of the Corporation. Since the time of Vesey there had been several occasions when Members had abused their position in order to benefit themselves and their close friends and relatives. Discontent in the 1780's and 1790's reached the point where a group of townsfolk, aggrieved at the mismanagement of the town's affairs, sought redress through the law courts. Their complaints covered such matters as felling timber without consent and stocking the Park with strangers' cattle. By 1792 they had obtained an injunction from the Court of Chancery in London which prevented further sales of timber by the Corporation and impounded money from earlier transactions.

Over thirty years passed before an understanding could be reached to resolve the impasse and allow satisfactory use to be made of the accumulated sum of £40,000, held by the Lord Chancellor in lieu of an agreement. In fact the first recorded mention of the legal battle did not appear until Friday 25th March 1808. The Corporation Minutes for that day note that the Committee, which they had established to negotiate with the Relators (the name given to the citizens who had been acting as 'informers to the Attorney-General' and thus begun the action), had submitted a plan to utilise the accrued monies to both parties.

A SCHEME EMERGES

One month later, April 1808, this paper was discussed at an Assembly held in the town's Moot Hall and it was recorded in its entirety in the Minute Book of the Corporation. It was given the title — 'A Scheme for the application of the increased Revenue of the Corporation of Sutton

Coldfield' and it lay down, in commendable detail, plans to reach a settlement.

It was proposed that —

> *"A Charity School . . . . be established in the Town of Sutton Coldfield for the moral and religious instruction of the Male and Female Children of the Poor Inhabitants of the Parish upon the new and improved System as recommended by Colquhoun and others or upon any other Plan which may be thought more eligible.'*

(Colquhoun was an 18th. century economist who believed that the education of the poor should properly consist of the 3Rs together with religion and the formation of habits of order and submission to their station in life — 'Progressives and Radicals in English Education 1750-1790' — W.A.C. Stewart).

A similar school was proposed for the hamlet of Hill. Interestingly it was also suggested that they employ 'proper persons to instruct Poor children under the age of 7 who live in the Parish', but who lived too far from the schools to attend. Money was set aside for the building and furnishing of the schools, the annual fuel bill and the salaries of the Masters or Mistresses. Furthermore regular attenders would be given a set of clothes annually for school wear; gross misbehaviour would be punishable by expulsion.

Another building was to be erected to house a School of Industry to educate 30 girls and to instruct them in such skills as sewing, spinning, knitting and in writing and arithmetic. The girls' clothing would be made by themselves and they would also be required to make garments for girls at the other schools. The young ladies would be expected 'to make up the Linnen to be lent or given to the Poor unmarried Women in Child bed and to knit stockings for the Boys'. For every child leaving school to enter an apprenticeship there would be a sum of £5-5-0 (£5.25) to be paid as a premium, to provide the necessary instruction into that trade. Numerous other proposals relating to the affairs of the town and ranging from the purchase of weighing machines to the provision of blankets for poor people were also included in the Scheme.

CONSULTATIONS AND DELIBERATIONS

Nine years passed during which the Relators and the Corporation argued over the many issues which divided them. Compromises were sought but not reached. In 1814 the Rector, John Riland, urged that the legal processes be terminated in order that a Scheme could be agreed and implemented. He failed.

At last, in May 1817, an acceptable position was reached and the Corporation Minutes could record 'that the Scheme for the appropriation of the increased revenues of the Corporation as this day settled shall be submitted to the approval of the Master (of the Court of Chancery).''

THE SCHEME OF 1817

When, then, were the final proposals accepted by both parties in the dispute? It was decided that a Charity School capable of giving 'moral and religious instruction to 100 male and female Children of the poor Inhabitants of this Parish upon the new and improved System as recommended by Dr. Bell and others or upon any other which may be thought eligible.' *

Likewise a similar school would be established to serve the hamlets of Hill and Little Sutton. In addition a preparatory School for 40 children living 'Beyond the Wood' (now called Walmley) would be erected to serve those children who lived at too great a distance to attend the alternative schools. The School of Industry would be housed in the Town School. By using timber from the Park it was anticipated that the schools could be built for a sum of £1,200. The salaries for the Masters of the Sutton and the Hill schools would be £40 annually; there would be £25 for the Mistress of the Walmley School while the Mistress of the School of Industry would receive £60, to allow her to obtain the services of an assistant. No child would be admitted before they were 6 years old and were to leave when they reached the age of 12 years. (The Court of Chancery preferred an upper limit of 14 but the Corporation had decided that this would have been unacceptable to the Court and had therefore lowered the upper age limit). It was anticipated that at least 240 children would attend the schools and to this end a sum of £2 per boy and £1 11s 6d (£1.57) per girl would be allowed for their clothing each year.

IMPLEMENTATION OF THE SCHEME

A year passed, presumably in further debate and argument, for the Scheme covered many other facets, other than educational provision for the

---

* Dr. Bell (1753-1832) advocated the Monitorial System of Teaching which used older pupils to teach the juniors. In this way he suggested that it would be possible to give the minimum amount of education to the greatest number of poor children in the most effective manner and in the shortest possible time.

The Almshouses and Town School superimposed on the survey of c. 1811.
The numbers refer to cottages as follows: No. 10 Widow Wilkins,
No. 11 Joseph James, No. 12 Bonell, No. 8 Widow Yates, No. 9 Thomas Nunn

Town, and in May 1818 the Corporation requested that Mr Joseph Bateman and Mr Thomas prepare plans for the buildings commensurate with the basic requirements in terms of accommodation and purpose. The Master of the Court of Chancery required Affidavits verifying the estimates of the building costs and the timber available to be cut for the purpose of erecting the schools.

THE TOWN SCHOOL

In May 1819 the Corporation agreed that two of their members would consult Mr Bateman, who was a Birmingham architect, about the Schools with a view to altering the plans or submitting fresh ideas to a future meeting. A survey revealed that the only suitable ground for the central schools was a site occupied by a row of cottages at the bottom of Mill Street which were in a poor state of repair. By the end of 1822 the occupiers of these hovels were approached to discover if they would give immediate possession to the Corporation. Mr Mendham and Mr Nicholson, members of the Society, discussed this proposal with Widow Wilkins, Joseph James, James Bonell, John Heath and Widow Yates. On 25th February 1823 these tenants were given notice to quit by Michaelmas. In May Mr Bateman was asked if he could value the timber from the Park needed to construct the schools and to 'point out where such timber ought to be fell and support the same by affidavit as required by the Master (of the Court of Chancery)'. The Warden and Society resolved on 16th September 1825 to undertake legal steps to gain possession of the cottages where the School and almshouses would be erected. They urgently requested that the Master in Chancery accept their choice of site so that there would be no further delay to the building programme. Just over a week earlier the various cottagers had again been interviewed and the responses they obtained were recorded in the Minutes.

Ann Wilkins said that she would not 'stir but her son said he would prevail on her provided they could be found another house'. Joseph James, Widow Heath, Widow Farmer and Thomas Norris were prepared to move, unlike Widow Yeates who would not leave.

The delays this caused led the Corporation to investigate the possibility of using temporary rooms for the schools until the buildings were complete. They resolved to use the lower room of the Town Hall for this purpose and by installing a partition they could ensure that both boys and girls could be taught simultaneously. On 9th November 1825 assistance was given in the form of temporary residences to some of the cottagers, and the offer of one of the new almshouses, as a means of inducing them to vacate the houses which were to be pulled down.

Detail of the Frontispiece — View of Sutton in 1840 — anonymous painting based on a sketch by Miss Bracken. Compare the elevation with that of Hill School (p.119), where the original block, with its four windows, pediment, and belfry is strikingly similar.

On November 21st 1825, the Committee 'appointed for the purpose of carrying into effect the Order for the application of the increased Revenue' met to consider the appointment of Masters and the numbers of children who would attend the Schools. They recommended that 'application be immediately made to the National Society for a Master duly qualified to superintend the establishment and progress of a school in Sutton' and that they 'make enquiry in the Parish to see if there is any fit person capable of undertaking the Duties of the said School who is willing to qualify himself for the system of education to be adopted, at the expense of the Corporation and according to the principles of the National School'. It was agreed to 'select' 40 boys and 40 girls initially to the schools and to pay the Mistress for the Town school a temporary salary of £30 per annum.

Once the Master was appointed for the Town school the Committee was very keen that 'he should be directed to take charge of the Boys' Sunday School and to select from it such Boys as he deems most competent to assist him in the establishment of the National School in Sutton'. (This recommendation was unacceptable to the Corporation, however).

It was felt important to elect a Committee which would be responsible for the management of the Schools and that only books approved by the National Society should be purchased.

On November 26th temporary appointments were made. William Felton was chosen to be the 'Schoolmaster for the intended temporary School in the Town till the School is built if he behaves himself properly and with the understanding that if he proves properly qualified he will be continued'. The Corporation further insisted that he should visit several schools in the district to gain experience and qualifications and agreed to pay him £40 a year whilst he undertook this task. A Mrs Shardlow was chosen as the Mistress of the Temporary Girls' School, to be retained if she were able to prove herself adequate for the task.

The children who would attend the schools were to be chosen on December 5th., in order that the temporary schools could commence teaching them on January 1st 1826. In the meantime instructions were issued to prepare the lower room in the Town Hall to accommodate them. When December 5th arrived the Warden and Society had second thoughts on the selection process and decided, instead, to have a Notice read out in Church and also placed upon the Church doors. It said — 'The inhabitants of this Parish who wish their Children to be admitted to the Charity Schools are to give the names and ages of all their Children at the Town Hall on Tuesday next. Ten o'clock'.

By December 14th the lists of children ready to be elected to the Schools were produced and submitted to the appointed Committee. On Christmas Eve the names children were accepted and the Sergeants (Corporation officials) were asked to inform the parents that the children should attend school on 23rd January 1826. At last the many years of argument were finally to end as the schools opened their doors for the first time.

A copy of the Town Schools' Admitance Register survives from this time and provides a wealth of information regarding the boys who attended the School during the early 19th century. On that first day 39 boys were admitted from the following parts of Sutton —

Sutton	25
Sutton Park	2
Brick Kiln Lane	3
Blabbs	2
Mr Oughton's Mill	2
Penns	2
K.C. Lane	1
Thimble End	1
Wyld Green (sic)	1

The occupations of the fathers were also recorded. The largest group of parents were labourers of whom there were 19. The remainder included a Spade Maker, 2 Gun Barrel Borers, 2 Tailors, Cow Leech (physician), Mason, 2 Wire Drawers, Sawyer, Shoe Maker, Park Keeper, Blacksmith, Grinder, Stock Weaver, Accountant and a Carpenter. One child was an orphan whilst another had only his mother to look after him.

The Corpration Minutes fail to mention this historic occasion — the fruition of years of argument, rancour and debate between many of the town's more prominent citizens. Yet it must have been with some considerable pride that these worthy gentlemen witnessed, albeit in temporary rooms, the opening of the Charity Schools.

In February agreements with the Master and Mistresses were finalised and Rules and Regulations were approved. The clothing to be provided by the Corporation was also agreed. Boys would wear a blue cloth jacket and trousers, together with shirt, stockings, woollen cap and shoes. The girls would have a blue cotton frock, straw bonnet and blue ribbon, together with shoes and stockings. Subsequently they were allowed a cloak. These decisions affected the local economy for it was an important condition that the tailors and shoemakers employed would 'be Master workmen resident in this Parish'.

For some time the Ladies Committee had been responsible for organising a Sunday School and the gentlemen of the Corporation thought it right and proper to suggest that they should be approached in case they could suggest improvements to the National School, as it was called sometimes. In the meantime the Sunday School continued to make use of an upper room in the Town Hall for their meetings. The Rector kindly agreed to purchase books and other items from the Society for Promoting Christian Knowledge at a cost of £28 11s 5d for which he received a 'check' in May 1826. Trees already felled were to be sold at an auction organised by Mr Solomon Smith and the proceeds used for building the Schools and the Almshouses. Some corrections were made to the plans and a sum of £1500 was set aside for the building of both the Town and the Hill Schools. A further sum of £250 10s 0d (£250.50) was to be spent on providing the necessary timber. The sloping nature of the ground on which Town School was to be erected meant additional finance and it was decided that this should be paid out of the general account and then reimbursement would be sought from the Accountant General, who was overseeing the Corporation finances.

It was found necessary to approach the Court of Chancery for more money to cover 'extra improvements and work done and to be done at

Great Sutton School — £476-6-0 (476.30)
The School at Hill — £359-16-10 (359.84)
The School Beyond the Wood and Walmley — £67-18-10 (£67.00)
& Church accommodation—£300-0-0(£300)

The latter item was to fund the decision by the Warden & Society to ask Mr Bateman, the architect, to prepare plans and estimates for the cost of enlarging the North and South Galleries in Holy Trinity Church to accommodate the children when they attended services. It was originally intended that there would be 'stone staircase communicating therewith or in such other manner that may appear to him (Mr Bateman) better for the accommodation of the said children'. When completed in 1828 they in fact appeared to have been given an iron staircase and entry to the galleries was through small doors placed into the east wall of the church. They remained in use until 1858 when they were removed.

HILL SCHOOL

Whilst the Town School was being established the Corporation took similar trouble with its other proposed schools. One of its members, Mr Kempson, was asked in 1822 to ascertain whether the Warden and Society owned any suitable land in Hill and on 18th December 1822 it was agreed

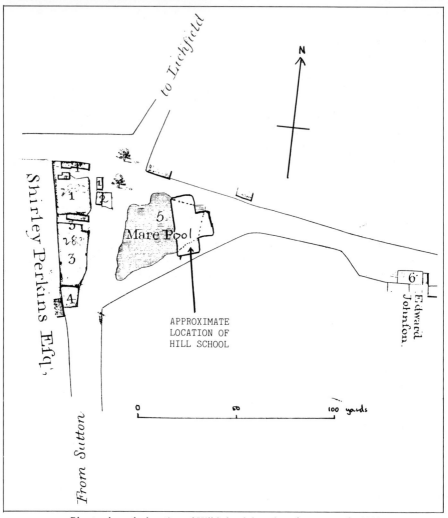

Plan to show the location of Hill School, based on the survey of c.1811

'that a piece of land at Mare Pool part of the Waste containing more than a rood situate between Mare Green and Little Sutton be the place recommended for building the proposed Charity School upon in that Quarter'.

In 1825 the site was defined as 'a part of the Waste upon Mare Geeen between the Meer and a Mefsuage or Tenement belonging to Mr Christopher Lucas'. It was felt that a temporary school for 25 boys and 25 girls could be established with the Mistress being paid £30 per annum.

Hill School, 1988

The first Master and Mistress were Mr and Mrs Daniel Aulton and they were appointed, subject to them promising that they were qualified for the task, at a much enhanced salary of £60. An agreement was signed which outlined the terms of their engagement. They were provided with accommodation by the Corporation, who agreed to rent for £10 a year, two cottages belonging to Mr Solomon Smith, situated between Four Oaks and Hill. It was this gentleman who was responsible for the school's construction.

The School still stands and a visit to it will discover the stone tablet which the various schools had built into their walls at the time of their completion. It reads 'Corporation School erected A.D. 1826'. Although many changes have been made to the building it is not too difficult to identify its original appearance.

WALMLEY SCHOOL

Originally, in 1822, it was proposed to construct this school on a piece of land owned by a Henry Brookhouse but, by the end of the year, it was felt that a parcel of land in Thimble End, the property of Mr Webster, was more suitable. In 1825 the Corporation proposed that it should be built on 'a small field occupied by Mr Webster on the South East Side of Signal Hayes field being the uppermost of the Crofts called Breedens Croft containing

One acre one rood and thirty nine perches'. As with the other schools it was felt desirable to establish a temporary school until the permanent school could be built. Only 10 boys and 10 girls would be 'elected' and the Mistress would be paid £15 per annum.

A Mrs Thomas Short was appointed initially and she agreed to educate the children in her own house temporarily, subject to any necessary alterations being undertaken. The builder of the new school was Mr Holbeche of Maney and he signed the draft agreement to construct it in May 1826.

Mrs Short was replaced in February 1827 by Sarah Ann Adams, daughter of Jane Adams who owned a shop in Maney. She was given the opportunity to rent, at a fair value, the remainder of the field on which the school had been erected, if she so wished.

The building still stands and can be seen adjacent to the new housing estate near the junction of Signal Hayes Road and Webster Way. It is set back some way from the road but still retains much of its original design, including its well.

CONCLUSION

By June 1827 the agreements between the Corporation and the teachers had been signed and the remaining vacancies for the children were filled up. At last the schools were established and operating. The control of them was placed in the hands of a School Committee, accountable to the Corporation and ultimately to the townspeople. Between 1826 and 1886, when Municipal reform led to the abolition of the Warden and Society, immense expansion of educational opportunities for local children took place as the population of the town grew. It is hoped that a further paper will be produced in due course covering the first sixty years of the Sutton Coldfield Municipal Charity Schools.

Sources
The Warden and Society Minutes 1723-1832.

The Anchorage Road Estate:

Late Nineteenth Century Residential development in Sutton Coldfield

By Janet Lillywhite

DURING THE SECOND HALF of the Nineteenth Century the population of Sutton Coldfield began to increase rapidly, rising from 4,574 in 1851 to 14,624 by the turn of the Century. This increase was mainly due to the town's development as a residential suburb for Birmingham and this article attempts to show something of the nature and timing of residential development during this period.

It was the enclosure movement of 1824 which paved the way for housing development by establishing the ownership of land, particularly on the commons and waste and discouraging the growth of poor squatter settlement in the parish. Some of the first evidence we have of land being sold for housing as opposed to agricultural use dates from this time when the Commissioner for Enclosure, Mr Harris, advertised ten acres of land fronting Chester Road for sale in 1826 specifically as building lots. Other important contributing factors were the developing rail links with Birmingham and Walsall and the town's attraction as a pleasant healthy neighbourhood separated from but easily accessible to the nearby industrial towns.

The positive benefit of a healthy rural surrounding was one which was actively promoted during this time. The Medical Officer of Health's reports show that Sutton had the enviable reputation of being one of the healthiest parts of Warwickshire. The infant mortality rate was amongst the lowest in the country and the general health of the town was good. In 1895 there was not a single death from smallpox, scarlet fever, diphtheria, typhoid fever or measles and by 1890, Bostock Hill, the Medical Officer of Health, could report that

> "*a sanitary condition had been obtained comparable with that of any health resort in the kingdom* [1]"

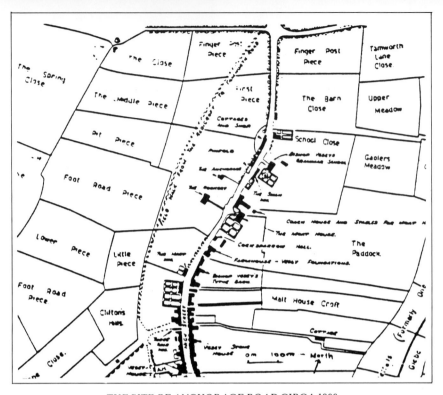

THE SITE OF ANCHORAGE ROAD CIRCA 1800
The field walk from Tamworth Road to Reddicroft formed the line of
Anchorage Road. The 'Anchorage' and the 'Rookery' were both built circa 1720.
The first sale of land on the Anchorage Estate was on 19 July 1870. The field
known as Foot Road Piece was advertised as the 'Rookery Field Estate', the
remaining fields Pit Piece, the Middle Piece, the Close, Finger Post Piece,
First Piece and Pinfold forming the 'Anchorage Estate'. (Map reproduced by
kind permission of N.G. Evans).

So it is not surprising that wealthy manufacturers and business men from Birmingham should wish to live here. G.B. St. Clair brought his young family to Sutton in the 1850's in order to

> *"educate them here and let them breathe your pure air and*
> *look upon your beautiful town and stroll through your*
> *splendid park"* [2]

One of the immediate effects of the increase in population was that new roads were laid out and new houses built. The first Ordnance Survey maps published in 1889 show fifteen new streets [3] mostly near the town centre, but there was also development at Wylde Green, where Station Road was laid out in 1860 with the coming of the railway, and a number of new villas had been built on the Birmingham and Lichfield roads. Victoria Road was developed in 1888 and the first houses on the Four Oaks Estate were built in 1892. During the 1880's some forty to fifty new houses were built each year and by the last five years of the Century this had increased to an average of nearly 300 houses a year.

The development of Anchorage Road is a good example of the speculative nature of the housing development that took place at this time. Evidence for the nature of this and other development comes from a number of sources, such as Auctioneers' Bills [4] which show where land was being sold for building purposes and the perceived attraction of the area. The Rate Books give annual details of owners and occupiers of buildings, but the

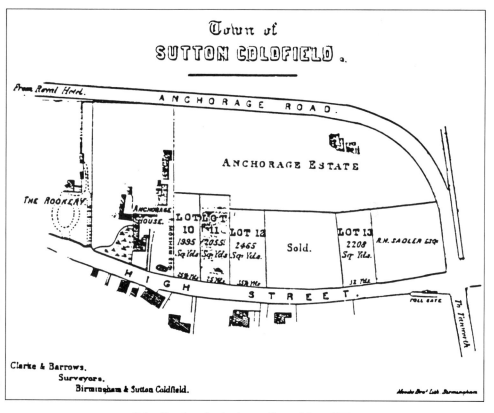

Sale of land on the Anchorage Estate 7 June 1871
The second sale of land on the Anchorage Estate shows the road laid out and
the first two houses, numbers 9 and 11 already built.

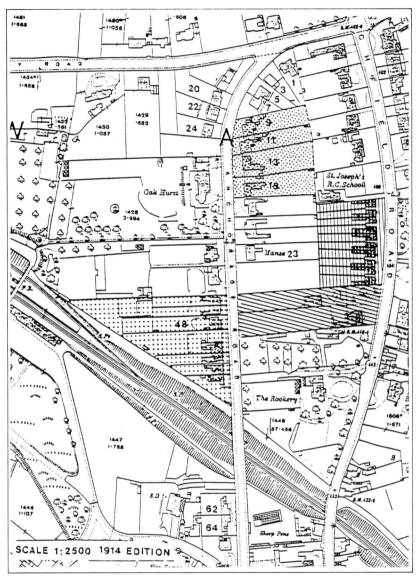

Map of Anchorage Road, showing the houses referred to

KEY

 THE ANCHORAGE

 WELLINGTON TERRACE
COMPLETED BY 1885

THE FIRST FOUR HOUSES
TO BE BUILT

LAND SOLD TO JOHN CANT

124

most valuable source of information comes from the building plans. After 1885 when Sutton Coldfield gained its municipal charter any person intending to build had to submit detailed building plans to the Borough Surveyor to ensure that the standard of construction conformed to the local bye-laws [5]. These plans provide detailed evidence of the pattern of development and of the architects, builders and character of the houses built. Lastly, the census returns can be used to give details of the people who lived in the houses — their place of birth, family size and social standing.

The Rate Books and Auctioneers' Bills show fairly conclusively that Anchorage Road was laid out in early 1870 and that it followed the line of an old footpath from Tamworth Road to the Reddicroft. The key to the development of the road lay in the ownership of a house known as 'The Anchorage' on the site of the present fire station. The 1868 Rate Book names the owner of the house and surrounding land as the Rev. C.B. Greatrex, but in 1869 the owner was R.H. Sadler, a local solicitor who lived in High Street.

Richard Sadler bought 'The Anchorage' as a building investment and in July 1870 the house and surrounding land with Anchorage Road laid out were advertised for sale in twenty six building lots by Clarke and Barrows, auctioneers of Birmingham. The auctioneers catalogue praises the advantages of the site which is

> *"situated on a dry gravelly sub-soil, with good slopes for drainage, commands extensive and beautiful views over Sutton Park and neighbourhood and comprises the most desirable and healthy situation in the Parish of Sutton Coldfield for Suburban Residence of a Superior Class, with easy access by Rail and Road to and from Birmingham"*

Richard Sadler obviously intended the land to be developed as a middle class road, and imposed quite stringent conditions on development

> *"No Dwelling House shall be of less cost and value, exclusive of outbuildings than £500. No manufacture nor any noxious, dangerous or offensive process shall be carried on upon any lot sold"*

It was quite usual at this time to impose restrictions on development in order to enhance the social standing of an area. The Four Oaks Estate had similar conditions including one to prevent the land being used 'for the sale or supply of victuals or as an Hotel' and another to prevent the development of semi-detached houses.

No. 5 Anchorage Road

By 1871 Richard Sadler had sold Anchorage House to Thomas Moxham a Gun Maker from Aston who, according to the 1871 census came to live there with his wife and five children. The first four houses in Anchorage Road (numbers 9 to 15) were built by 1872 and occupied by 1873. They set the standard for development in the road being large double fronted detached houses, with a rateable value of £51.

It was usually felt that to be a success building development needed a railway station, a church and a park nearby and Anchorage Road had all three. So it is rather surprising to find that no more houses were built for sixteen years, until 1888. The initial reason is not difficult to find. The Midland railway was opened in 1879, so access to Anchorage Road, from the Southern town side would have been difficult if not impossible while the cutting was excavated and the bridge built. But Richard Sadler had been quite astute in laying out the road when he did, because he would have received compensation for the land he lost, which would have been rated as building rather than agricultural land, and the Midland Railway would have paid for the cost of the bridge. However, he was not idle during these sixteen years and turned his attention to the land fronting Lichfield Road and built Wellington Terrace, which was completed by 1885.

In 1888 development started again in Anchorage Road. John Cant, an estate agent of Aston, bought a section of land on the West of the road adjacent to the railway and built five houses in the next seven years. One plot of land he leased to Joseph Fray who built one pair of semi-detached houses in 1896, but the last plot remained vacant until 1913.

Building continued at a steady pace and by the first World War all but two of the houses were built, but architecturally the style changed. The early houses, those built for John Cant and Joseph Fray, were Victorian Gothic in style with ornate gables, porches and bay windows, but by the turn of the Century the influence of the Arts and Crafts movement can be seen, with their simpler lines, white stucco walls and small lead paned windows. Some of these houses were designed by local architects such as J. Titley (Numbers 62 and 64) and Marston and Healey (Numbers 20,22,24). Others were built by more well known architects such as Bateman and Bateman who designed numbers 5 and 7, which are semi-detached houses designed to look like one house. 'The Manse' (Number 23) reflects a more formal style of Arts and Crafts architecture and was designed by Crouch and Butler for George Lowe who owned 'Oak Hurst', the largest house in the road.

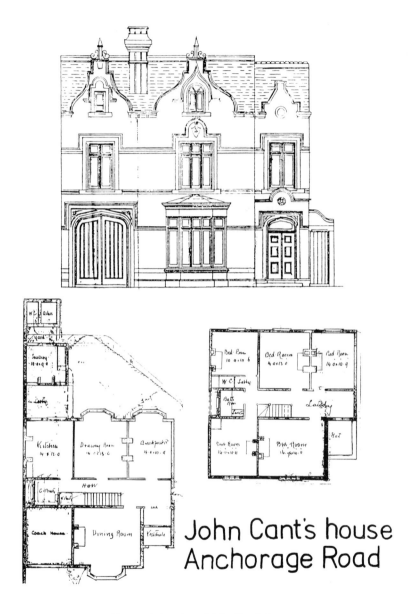

John Cant's house
Anchorage Road

Plans and elevation of John Cant's house

The manner in which housing developed in Anchorage Road was very typical of the pattern of development in Sutton Coldfield at the time. Most land was leased or sold in small building plots providing land for between two and six houses. Once the houses were built they were usually leased, very few houses were owner occupied. It was quite common for the owner to live in one house and let the others, so John Cant lived in one of the houses he built, while George Dugard who built two detached houses 'Rockingham' and 'Melrose' (Numbers 40 and 42), lived in one and let the other. The Rate Books show that there was a high turnover in housing, relatively few people living in the same house for more than two or three years.

There is no direct evidence for the cost of land in Anchorage Road, but building land fronting Lichfield Road was sold for about £200 an acre in 1886. Smaller three bedroomed villas, such as those in Victoria Road and Station Road, had a rateable value of £18 and would have let for about £25 a year and houses in Anchorage Road would let for between £75 and £100. There is some evidence that conditions were imposed on leases in the same way as they were on the initial development. A local wine merchant, E.H. James, let two houses in Four Oaks Road and imposed quite stringent conditions to protect his own interests and the general standards of the area. The outside of the house had to be painted once every third year 'in two coats of good oil colour'. There were clauses prohibiting trade, business or underletting and the trees in the garden were to be 'nourished and supported' and not cut unless consent in writing was granted.

The people who lived in Anchorage Road were typical of the middle classes living in Sutton Coldfield at the time. In 1881, the latest date for which the detailed census enumerators returns are published, there were only three houses occupied and only one of the original four occupants of the road still lived there. This was Elizabeth Keeling, a teacher who kept a school. She lived in the house with her mother and two other teachers, one of whom came from Germany. There were eight scholar boarders, ranging in age from nine to sixteen years, and all but one, who came from Leicester, lived in or near Sutton. Miss Keeling also employed a resident cook and housemaid.

One of the other houses was occupied by Jane Evans, a widow from Ilkeston in Nottinghamshire, whose income was said to be derived from land. She lived with her unmarried son Walter who was a clerk to a wine merchant and they had one resident servant. The third house was occupied by Frederick Hathaway from Walsall, his wife Annie, their twelve year old niece and a servant. Mr Hathaway was a wholesale manufacturer in saddlery goods employing thirty girls, fifteen men and six boys. So it is possible that he was following the fashion of the time, and like G.H. St. Clair and Thomas Moxham leaving his house adjacent to his factory for the more rural surroundings of Sutton Coldfield and using the recently built Midland Railway to commute to Walsall.

The houses in Anchorage Road reflected a middle class standard of life. Number 48, a detached house designed by Roger Harley of Birmingham and built in 1891 is typical. The plan and elevation show that on the ground floor are a drawing room, dining room and breakfast room; the dining room some sixteen by fourteen feet is the largest room in the house,

Villa Residences, Numbers 52 and 54 Anchorage Road
The houses were built in 1896 for Joseph Fray of Victoria Road, Sutton Coldfield. Constructed of brick walls and slate roof, each house had a dining room, drawing room, kitchen and scullery with three bedrooms and bathroom on the first floor, attic rooms and cellar. Water supply came from the South Staffordshire Water Board. The right hand house, in which Joseph Fray most likely lived had a coach house. The architects were Matthews and Putchar of Cherry Street Birmingham and the builders were J. Turville and Sons of High Street, Sutton Coldfield.

reflecting Victorian middle class social values [6]. At the front there was an integral coach house; a well to do family in the 1890's would have expected to own their own coach but they would have hired horses when necessary. Upstairs there were five bedrooms and a bathroom and a further two bedrooms in the attic for the servants. In the basement there were three cellars, one for coal, one for wine and one for beer. The rateable value of this house was £47 and in 1894 it was owned by John Cant and leased to John Matthews.

Although not all new development in the town consisted of the middle class housing typical of Anchorage Road, it was the dominant influence on the town's development during a time when Sutton Coldfield was changing from an agricultural and small scale industrial town to a residential suburb.

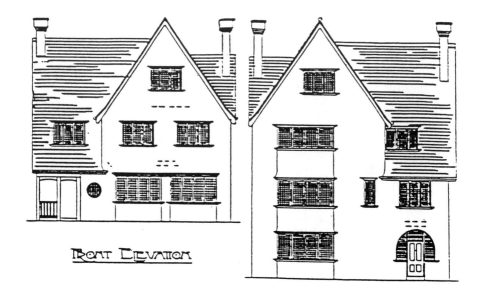

Front Elevation

Back Elevation

Number 24 Anchorage Road
The owner of this house which was built in 1903 was Ernest Healey, a partner in the local architects firm of Marston and Healey who designed the house. On the ground floor was a large hall with bay window, drawing room, dining room, kitchen and scullery. There were three bedrooms and bathroom on the first floor and two attic rooms. The steep slope of the land allowed a well lit basement billiard room to be included at the rear.

The two elements continued to exist side by side; a contemporary report describes the population as consisting of

> *"the poorer artisans employed in making wire or tools, or agricultural labourers, and the wealthier tradesmen and manufacturers with business in Birmingham"*[7]

But the general economic depression of the 1880's and the positive promotion of the town's residential function helped to bring about the decline of traditional employment and by 1892 Bostock Hill could say that despite the 'considerable depression in trade and agriculture' there was 'very important evidence of growth and prosperity' in the town shown by the number of new houses built.

REFERENCES

1. Bostock Hill. Medical Officer of Health's annual reports 1886—Ref. SH45.12
2. 1854. Proceedings of Public meeting on Clifton Hill. Monday 10th April 1854.
3. A survey map for Sutton exists for 1856 and between then and 1889 the following streets were laid out:
   Highbridge, Station, Vesey, Eastern and Western Roads, Anchorage Road, Tudor Hill, Richmond Road, Clifton and Somerville Roads, Manor Road, Avenue Road, Newhall and Queen Street, Midland Road.
4. 'Auctioneers Bills for Staffordshire, Warwickshire and Worcestershire' (ref. 264926) and 'A Collection of Auctioneers Bills' (ref. 511833). Birmingham Reference Library.
5. Rate Books. Registers and individual plans are kept in Sutton Coldfield Reference Library.
6. A Social History of Housing 1815-1970. John Burnett. Methuen 1978. pages 94-117.
7. Sidwell Papers. Ref. 624.509. Birmingham Reference Library.

The Early Years of the Sutton Coldfield Volunteer Fire Brigade 1886—1907

by David Chubb

THE PUBLIC HEALTH ACT OF 1875 caused many councils to form proper municipal fire brigades; 'others wheeled out their old manual engines, dusted them off, and persuaded a few local volunteers to man them'[1]. However, it did not have any effect at all in Sutton Coldfield, because the council did not consider itself to have any public health responsibilities under the old Charter then in force. The new Charter of 1885, however, meant that the council had to consider what to do, and the existing arrangements were found wanting.

The Sutton Coldfield Volunteer Fire Brigade was set up at a public meeting held on 21st July 1886. Alderman Ansell presided and there were about 50 people present. Alderman Ansell said that the Council had recently undertaken the formation of a volunteer fire brigade and had voted £350 for the purpose. He stated that they 'had an engine and upon one occasion when it was wanted it was found to be full of potatoes (laughter)'.

The General Purposes Committee had suggested the provision of a manual engine and he thought that 12-15 men ought to be sufficient together with a captain and a lieutenant. There was, he said, no question of a paid brigade because that would mean an increase in the rates. They proposed to furnish each volunteer with a cap, a tunic, a belt, a pair of trousers and some boots — 'That in itself would amount to something like £5—£10 per man'. A Mr Parr moved that the meeting approve the suggestion of the town council, and it was carried unanimously. Alderman Ansell said that the officers of the brigade would be appointed by the volunteers and the committee of the council; the names of 27 volunteers were sent in.

At a meeting of the General Purposes Committee on 30th July 1886, the 27 volunteers were invited and their particulars noted. The Committee then

133

The Shand, Mason Fire Engine outside the first fire station

selected 12 firemen and 6 supernumeraries — they were: John Fletcher, Borough Surveyor; Charles Stewart from Coleshill Street; Charles Cole, a carpenter from Duke Street; Charles Scott; Charles Roper from Coleshill Street; Frank Parr, a china and glass dealer who lived at 18, Parade; John Whittaker from Newhall Street; John Weaver; Thomas Trappett, billposter and Town Crier from Lower Parade; Richard Steventon, a plumber and gas fitter from The Parade; Tom Hardy from Holland Street; Alfred Woodcroft, a wood-turner, who lived in Coleshill Street. The Supernumeraries were: Joseph Horton; John Bickley junior; Thomas Gould; Walter Smith; Charles Huckle; and H. Weston. In August the Borough Surveyor, John Fletcher, was elected captain of the fire brigade with Charles Stewart as his lieutenant.

Some comments by the writer of a column in the Sutton Coldfield and Erdington Times, calling himself 'Willie Westlake', suggest that some people found the V.F.B. a source of amusement. He wrote complaining of 'the levity being displayed in connection with the Volunteer Fire Brigade for our Royal Borough' — he said that it was a mistake to suppose that their work would be confined to rick or haystack fires; the Brigade 'will doubtless be called upon at times to put out fires at business places, private dwellings and so forth, and then it will be found that work will be placed beyond fun.' He concluded his column with these stern words: 'It is time all this levity was dropped and the duties looked upon from a much more serious standpoint'.

Mr Charles Browning became captain of the Volunteer Brigade later the same year. He was at that time the station master at the Town Station of the Midland Railway in Midland Drive (where he issued the first tickets on 1st July 1879). The Fire Station was situated in the Town Hall (now the Masonic Buildings) in Mill Street; on 18th October 1886 the subcommittee had accepted the tender of Messrs. Shand, Mason & Co. for a fire engine and appliances at a cost of £179-5-0, and this was kept in the fire station, but there were no horses. Horses were made available to the brigade by local tradesmen, who were paid 15/- per horse for their hire. They were John Holford, cab proprietor of High Street, James Bull, Samuel Swinburn, dairyman of Park Road, and William Allport, cab proprietor and furniture remover, of Station Street. This system was not without its difficulties; in his report of a hedge fire dated 30th August 1887, Captain Browning says 'The delay in getting to the fire was owing to the difficulty in obtaining horses, Mr Holford who supplies horses for the engine only having one fit to work and Mr Swinburne who assists him having both his horses out. We had to procure one from Mrs Archer.'

The first meeting of the Fire Brigade and Hackney Carriage Committee was on the 18th December 1888, with Alderman Read in the Chair. Prior to this time Fire Brigade matters had been dealt with by the General Purposes Committee. Captain Browning submitted his first annual report to this committee in June 1889, detailing the five fires attended during the year, being two house fires, one chimney fire, one hedge fire and one gorse fire in Sutton Park; none of them were 'serious'.

The first reported house fire attended by the V.F.B. was at George Whitlock's (photographer), 3, Park Road, on 14th June 1887 — on arrival they found that the fire had been extinguished. The Brigade's first drill had taken place earlier that same month, using their new Shand Mason fire

SUTTON COLDFIELD, ERDINGTON,

BILLPOSTING...

...BILLPOSTING.

T. TRAPPETT,

Billposter,

LOWER PARADE,

SUTTON COLDFIELD,

Begs to inform the Inhabitants of

Sutton Coldfield, Four Oaks, Erdington, Coleshill,

and the outlying districts, that he will be pleased to contract for work in all its various branches.

DISTANCE NO OBJECT.

PRIVATE STATIONS SECURED.

Estimates Supplied Free.

SPECIALITY—SALES ATTENDED ON COMMISSION.

Fireman Trappett was town crier and bill-poster as well

136

engine. This is the machine in the photographs of the fire station and the jubilee procession. By the end of that month the V.F.B. had 12 suits of clothes which cost £28-17-7.

At this time there was no telephone at the fire station and the alarm was raised by ringing the alarm bell; any firemen in the vicinity would rush to the station, and the bell would also alert the owners of the horses used to pull the engine that their services would be required. This system was not foolproof, however, as Captain Browning reported in April 1889: "owing to the church bells ringing during the time the fire bell was being rung attendance of firemen was only two besides myself and no horses arrived owing to the same cause". The horse owners caused Captain Browning problems too. He reported in April 1890 that Mr Swinburne refused to allow his horse to pull the engine with one of Mr Bull's horses: "I attempted to take the horse from him and as he would not leave go the Horse I called the police Sargeant to my assistance and I again took possession of the horse".

The V.F.B. seems to have attended remarkably few fires in Sutton during these early years: five during the first year, six in the second and five in the third. Out of this total of sixteen fires, ten were house or chimney fires, three were rick fires, there was one hedge fire and two in the Park. The fourth annual dinner of the V.F.B., held on 12th February 1891 at the Museum Hotel, was interrupted by the fire bell. Captain Browning and some of the firemen left the dinner to attend to the fire, in a shed at Four Oaks; it did not take long to deal with this blaze, and the firemen were able to return to the festivities in time to hear Alderman Read sing his favourite song, 'The Star of Bethlehem'.

Section 66 of the 1875 Public Health Act required local authorities to provide and maintain water supplies for dealing with fires, and to provide marked hydrants in the street. However, for reasons of economy, a cheap but inefficient type of hydrant was often installed, and there was no standardisation. This lack of uniformity caused problems when brigades from another town were called to a fire and found that they could not connect up their hoses. By June 1897 there were 88 fire hydrants in Sutton. Later that year the Borough Surveyor produced a plan for a further 53 hydrants for the protection of 'the large number of buildings in course of erection in various parts of the Borough". (The population of Sutton increased from 8686 in 1891 to 14,264 in 1901).

In 1897 Mr Allport finished his contract for horsing the engine, and the horses were then supplied by the Highway Committee. This did not reduce the efficiency of the V.F.B., as Captain Browning was able to boast in April 1899 of "the average time in turning out to fires being 5 minutes, which cannot be beat by many other county Fire Brigades".

Captain Browning had been pressing for better equipment, and in 1900 the Fire Brigade Commitee agreed to make enquiries as to the capital cost of a steam fire engine and the annual maintenance costs etc. In September the Committee invited tenders, and in April 1901 the purchase of a 350 gallon steam fire engine from Messrs. Merryweather and Son at a price of £348/10/- and £89/16/- for hoses was approved. The engine was delivered on October 1st, and on November 9th 1901, at a ceremony at Moat House, the engine was formally christened 'Alexandra' (Queen Alexandra lent her name to a great many enterprises), by the Mayoress, Mrs Glover. In his speech, Councillor Sadler said of the Volunteer Fire Brigade: "It consisted principally of employees of the council and they must not expect too much of them, for whatever they did they did voluntarily". On behalf of the Committee and the Council he thanked them and expressed the hope that now they had a new engine they would attend regularly to their drill. "They had now an engine with which they could deal with any fire".

Diamond Jubilee procession, 1897, the VFB just turning out of High Street

The Merryweather Steamer outside the new fire station,
Captain Browning on the left

The Merryweather Sutherland Steamer had won the prize at the International Competition at the Crystal Palace in 1863. When the alarm went, the engineer would drop a match down the funnel to light the fire under the boiler. The fire was built upside-down, with coal at the bottom, wood in the middle, and kindling at the top, and as the engine raced through the streets the draught created would ensure a good heat from the firebox, heating the water to create steam to drive the powerful pumps; these pumps could maintain a steady jet 150 feet high through a 1.5 inch nozzle.

In October 1904, "The horses and appliances with the exception of the Manual which the Mayor kindly allowed me to place in his coach house were removed to their temporary quarters in the Anchorage Road", reported Captain Browning. These temporary quarters were the cottage, stable and coach house adjoining The Hollies, on the corner of Upper Clifton Road, and were needed when the old town hall and offices in Mill street were sold for £4150 early in 1904. The appliances remained in their temporary accommodation until the new fire station was opened on December 1st, 1905, by Councillor and Mrs J. Bamford. Councillor

Official opening of the fire station, King Edward Square
1st December 1905

Bamford, who was the Chairman of the Fire Brigade Committee, entertained the members of the fire brigade to supper that evening at the Royal Hotel. Captain Browning wrote "It is with great pleasure I report the opening of the new Fire Station on December 1st last by Mrs Bamford opening the doors with a silver key presented to her by his worship the Mayor Mr Councillor Sadler, and the Chairman Mr Councillor Bamford unveiling the brass memorial tablet inside the engine house. By the kind invitation of the Chairman the members of the Brigade in the evening were entertained at supper at the Royal Hotel which was greatly appreciated by us and we most cordially thank him".

The new fire station in King Edwards Square (vacated in 1963, now the Bedford Suite), consisted of an engine room, stabling for four horses, and a recreation room for the firemen. The clock tower was used for drying hoses, as an observation post, and for ventilation. Captain Browning lived in the new Town Hall as caretaker, and land below the fire station in Upper Clifton Street was set out as allotment gardens for the firemen.

On Tuesday 22nd August 1905, on their way to a practice drill, the hose carriage, drawn by two horses and carrying 10 men, mounted the bank in

Tamworth Road and turned onto its side. Fireman E.B. Higgs, who had been sitting on a plank placed across the side seats to provide extra seating, was trapped underneath. He had suffered four broken ribs, rupture of the lungs, and injuries to his right eye; he was taken by car to the General Hospital in Birmingham, but died the next morning of shock caused by these injuries.

The initial cause of the accident was ascribed by the driver to the bit of one of the horses becoming entangled in the polechain, causing the horses to swerve towards the bank. There was a suggestion that the brakes had not been applied in the proper manner, but at the inquest the jury returned a verdict of accidental death. However, the foreman reported that the jury were of the opinion that the vehicle used was not suitable for so many passengers and that the temporary seat ought not to have been there. The Fire Brigade Committee requested the Chief Officer of the Birmingham Fire Brigade to inspect the hose carriage. He reported on 21st September that the machine was trustworthy and similar to those in use by brigades in Belfast, Nottingham, and Birmingham; however, if an additional seat was required, he suggested it be made a permanent fixture, and he recommended that the brakes be made to act together rather than working separately.

Fireman Higgs was buried in Sutton Coldfield Cemetery. A relief fund was set up for his wife and six children, which realised £335/13/5; the Committee decided to disburse the money by an allowance of 15/- a week for the first year, 13/6 the second year, and 10/- a week thereafter.

In January 1907 one of the original members of the volunteer brigade, Lieutenant Stewart, resigned owing to advanced age, while Firemen Trappett and Steventon, who had attended no drills or fires for a year, were asked to hand in their uniforms. In his report (his 20th) presented in April 1907, Captain Browning stated that the number of turn-outs in the year, 17, was a record. 4 were to residences, 9 to the Park, 1 a field and hedge fire, and 3 to farm buildings, the average time of turning out being 5 minutes. There were now 225 hydrants in Sutton.

Captain Browning resigned his position as captain of the V.F.B. in March 1909, although he continued to act as the person in charge for another four years. A professional fireman, Mr W.H. Dean, was appointed in 1913; he was paid 30 shillings a week plus a house. Charles Browning continued his other duties as Sergeant-at-arms, Mayor's messenger, and Curator until July 1917; on his retirement he was granted a pension of 10 shillings per week. He died in March 1926 in his 80th year. His funeral was held at Erdington Parish Church on March 24th, when six firemen from Sutton acted as pallbearers; the wreath from the Corporation of Sutton Coldfield was inscribed 'In remembrance of long and devoted service as captain of the brigade'.

Notes.
1. HUGHES, Evan Green, *The Story of Firefighting,* Moorland, 1979.
2. Sources used throughout: Minutes of the Fire Brigade and hackney Carriage Committee; Minutes of the Finance Committee; Minutes of the General Purposes Committee; Annual Reports of the Captain of the Fire Brigade (Sutton Coldfield Borough Records at Sutton Reference Library); Sutton Coldfield and Erdington Times; all covering the period 1886-1907.

The Parade at the turn of the century.

Early days on The Parade

by Marian Frankling

THE ROAD WHICH WE KNOW TODAY as Sutton Parade was originally called The Dam. The Medieval Manor Mills were on the site of the present Knot Inn, and the mill pools were where the Gracechurch Centre now stands, being formed by a dam on the line of the present Lower Parade. In 1668 a great flood broke down the dam, completely draining the mill pool. The mill was eventually demolished, and by the beginning of the nineteenth century only the names of Mill Street and The Dam remained to show what had been.

In 1826 the road between Manor Hill and High Street was reconstructed to obtain a better level and a more direct line, by raising the turnpike road across the valley. The dam wall at the side of the new road was removed, but the new straight road on its causeway above the old dam soon became popularly known as The Dam.

In 1869 the land along The Dam became the subject of a 94-year lease, granted from March 25th (Lady Day) of that year; the land was part of the Manor Farm, owned by Captain Somerville. Even in 1869 there were some buildings along the dam, although the Centre was thought of as the Three Tuns in High Street. One building was at the junction with Manor Road, and was known as 'The Old Pie Shop'; its chimneys can be seen on Miss Agnes Bracken's 1840 sketch of Sutton. It was not demolished until 1913, and I was able to speak to people who remember it. One Sutton lady recalls that the shop window was on the Parade, but the pavement had been raised so that you had to look down to see into the shop, the entrance to which was down four steps, where there was a warning — 'bend or bump'. Once inside the shop, where cooked meats and pies were sold, you could only see the feet of people passing on the pavement.

An even older building, 'Yew Tree Cottage', stood on Lower Parade; its occupants in 1668 must have witnessed the great flood of that year. Five cottages nearby housed small businesses — the 1870 Directory lists a shoemaker, a plasterer, and a basket-maker. These cottages were

Winter on the Dam—Yew Tree Cottage is half-hidden behind the tree on the right.

demolished in 1937 to make way for Burton's mens wear shop. The Knot Inn was formerly called the Dog Public House, replacing an earlier pub known as 'The Dog in the Hole' or 'The Old Dog'; in 1870, the proprietor offered 'accommodation and stabling at very reasonable terms'.

The first building to be erected on the west side of the Dam after the granting of the lease was the Museum public house. This opened in 1870, with the address of Mill Street, although later it was in the Parade. On January 25th 1879 an item appeared in the gossip column of the Sutton News commenting on the new name conferred on the Dam in the circular of an enterprising tradesman — The Parade. The Editor commented that the new idea was pleasant, but that some people might object to the removal of an old landmark, should the Dam lose its original name. Two readers kept up a correspondence for several weeks one with the pseudonym 'Keep it dark' in favour of 'The Parade', while 'SJH' was very much against it. As no-one else seemed sufficiently interested to join in, the editor eventually declared the correspondence closed. Gradually the 'Parade' found favour with other tradespeople, and on May 5th 1880 M. Taylor of Malvern House, Sutton Coldfield, announced in the Sutton News that her millinery and fancy goods shop had opened on the Parade.

This Reproduction of the first (May 1880) Parade Advertisement appeared in the Centenary Saturday Edition of the 'Sutton News' 1979

The Olde Pie Shoppe, c.1900

The Parade at the turn of the century, looking West.

From then on other shops began to claim Parade addresses, and in Kelly's Directory for 1880 the following are listed on the Parade:

> Louis Bayliss, The Tripe House;
> John Arthur Draycott, Photographer:
> George Evans, Butcher;
> Alfred Williams, Grocer.

Building began at the Mill Street end, continuing during the 1880's and 1890's down the west side towards Manor Road. From time to time newspaper advertisements announced the opening of yet another Parade shop: on August 28th 1880 W. Crisp's boot and shoe stores (with sewing machines to sell or hire); April 1881 saw the opening of Dunn Brothers, merchant tailors; A.J. Rodway began business as a tailor and hatter in February 1882, but failed to prosper, being declared bankrupt in 1894; J. Harrison, butcher set up in June 1885, as did Ann Higgs, fruiterer; shortly afterwards came P. Bennett's Boot and Shoe Warehouse and J. Frank Parr, china, glass and earthenware all at Birmingham prices. By 1888 at least 20 businesses had opened on the Parade. While Parrs had souvenirs for the Sutton Park visitors, most of the trade was local; typical prices were: dress suit 63/- (Rodways), tea 2/- a pound (Pugh's), roasting cuts of beef 6d a pound (Eastman's).

As the Parade developed, the focal point of the town moved from High Street until the Parade itself became regarded as the centre of Sutton Coldfield. This was endorsed by the opening of the Wesleyan Methodist church in honour of Queen Victoria's golden jubilee in 1887 on the corner of Newhall Street (converted into the town's first public library in 1937). Other new establishments were a vet, a circulating library, and a dining room. In 1885 Evans the butcher stole a march on his competitors by purchasing the prime beast from the Christmas show, which had been owned by the Prince of Wales, enabling him to boast of having provided rump steak for the Royal household at Sandringham. *The Sutton Coldfield and Erdington Chronicle* carried a light-hearted account of 'progress' in the Royal Town in 1896: "We now have an establishment for the sale, hire and repair of bicycles, a van for the removal of furniture, and at the commencement of the new year, as a finishing touch to our progress, or rather moving off, we have a funeral establishment" (S.J. Bastable, 62, Parade).

The steady development of the Parade was not matched by improved services such as footpaths and sanitation. A Birmingham visitor wrote to the Sutton news in 1878 complaining of the filthy smells, contrasting the

AND DISTRICT DIRECTORY.

NEWHALL STREET.

FROM LOWER PARADE.

RIGHT SIDE.

Allsopp, Henry
Hartwell, Thomas
10 Vickers, George
12 Cassidy, Richard
14 Samwells, George
16 Higgs, —
18 Watton, Thomas H.
20 Wright, Thomas

LEFT SIDE.

7 Slarke, S.
9 Grimley, Joseph

11 Betts, Mrs.
13 Allsopp, George Henry
15 Goodenough, A.
17 Owen, W. A.
19 Whittacre, John
21 McCormack, S.
23 Hitchin, M.
25 Benton, R. W.
27 Middleman, Mrs.
29 Wheeler, Mrs.
31 Starkey, George
33 Carter, George

PARADE.

FROM MILL STREET.

RIGHT SIDE.

2 Richards, Harry (Museum Hotel)
4 Moreton, James
6 Glover, Thomas
8 **BAYLISS, LOUIS**, Tripe House *(see advt.)*
10 Eastmans Limited : A. F. Hastilow, *Manager*
12 Higgs, Mrs. Ann
14 Phillips, Caroline
16 **HAYNES, E.**, Stationer, News-agent, and dealer in Fancy Goods *(see advt.)*
18 **PARR, JOHN FRANK**, Glass and China Merchant
20 Harrison, Frederick
22 Watton, Joshua
24 **FELTON, CLEMENT**, Ironmonger *(see advt.)*
26 Coles, Thomas
28 Clowes, Thomas William
30 Wheeley, Frederick
34 Evans, George Stokes
36 Crane, William Clifton
38 Grice, Joseph
40 Hall, Mary Hannah
42 **WODHAMS, LAWRENCE HENRY**, Grocer
44 Smith, J. Oldham
46 and 48, Brittain, H. A.
50 Attkins and Son
52 Harpur, Mrs. E. J.
54 Stone, W. H.
56 Pugh and Henson

58 Hodgkinson, Robert
60 **BAYLISS, E. R. J.**, Cycle Maker *(see advt.)*
60 Le Tellier, Joseph
62 Bastable, S. J.
64 Mason, Thomas
66 Grove, Mrs. C.
72 Harston and Sons
74 Salt, Henry
76 Nutt, Mrs. E.
78 Wood, A. E.
80 Reeves, Joseph
82 Sudbury, Miss A. J.
84 Whitney, Mrs.
86 Sims, —
Smith, W. A.
Jones, W. T.
Haywood, E. H.
Wakefield, George
Winspur, Mrs. (Bridge House)
Cole, F. W.

LEFT SIDE.

VALLANCE, THOMAS, Photographer *(see advt.)*
Dain, Frederick Sydney
Here is Wesleyan Church.
G. J. Ayre, B.A., *Minister.*
Here is Newhall Street.
83 Fawdry Brothers
85 **STEVENTON, RICHARD**, Plumber and Gas Fitter *(see advt.)*
87 Adams, Thomas

PARK (THE).

Bowers, William (Bracebridge Cottage)
Evans, William (Banner's Lodge)
Foden, James (Streetly Lodge)
Nicholls, Charles (Rowton Cottage)
Perry, William (Longmore Farm)

Riddell, Edward
Townshend, Charles (Hollyhurst Cottage)
Wood, Albert (Midland Lodge)
Yarwood and Keeling (Powell's Pool)

A page of the 1900 Directory

invigorating air of the Park with the unhealthy state of the town. Another correspondent complained of the poor state of the roads and footpaths — the cobblestone footpaths were made of 'petrified kidneys', almost impossible to walk on, making it preferable to wade through the mud of the 'horse road'. The Parade was described as one of the most unsightly streets of the borough in 1887, waste land on the eastern side being a receptacle for all kinds of rubbish — "how nice it would be if this could be converted into a nice crescent with a fountain and seats". By 1890, partly at the initiative of the Parade ratepayers, proper sewers had been laid and the pavement had been asphalted.

The early years of the 20th century were recalled in an interview with Miss Harpur, who lived at the family business at 52 Parade from 1899 to 1910 — there were four other children in the family. The attic and basement were the haunt of the children indoors, while the Park and the Ebrook, which then ran at the bottom of the gardens of the Parade houses, were the outdoor attractions. Returning from the brook on one occasion with a jar of minnows, the jar was accidentally dropped, and the shopkeeper came out

The Parade at the turn of the century, with the Wesleyan Church on the right, which became Sutton Library in 1937. Since the new Library was opened it has become a church again.

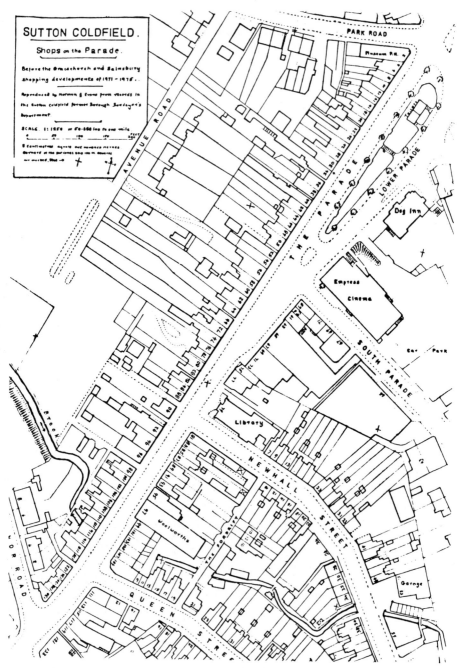

Plan of the Parade shops. The numbering corresponds to that in the 1900 Directory, except that numbers above 86 had either not be allocated or not yet built by 1900.

to clear the mess; sweeping the pavement and clearing the snow outside the shop was part of the routine. 52, Parade continued to be known as Harpur's long after the Botteleys took it over, and in 1970 Miss Harpur was invited back to look around her old home again before it was demolished.

102 The Parade was built between 1902 and 1912, but was similar in construction to the other shops there. Mr John Dodd lived there for many years, and gave a description of the accommodation. The building combined shop and living accommodation for the shopkeeper; this consisted of a kitchen and larder below pavement level, lit by small panes of glass below the level of the shop window, and glass tiles in the floor at the entrance to the shop. To the rear of these was a dining room with french windows opening onto a small bricked yard with coal house and WC. There was also a scullery at this level, with a staircase up to the shop at Parade level, and then the sitting room and landing on the floor above that. A further staircase led up to the second floor, containing two attic bedrooms.

102 The Parade had been established as an ironmongers from the outset, by a Mr Walker, being re-opened by Dodd's in 1919 after having been a soldiers' canteen during the Great War. When the 94-year lease expired in 1963 the shops were able to continue in business for a few years, until the construction of the Gracechurch Centre necessitated their demolition, Dodd's being one of the last to close in 1974.

The Parade 1948

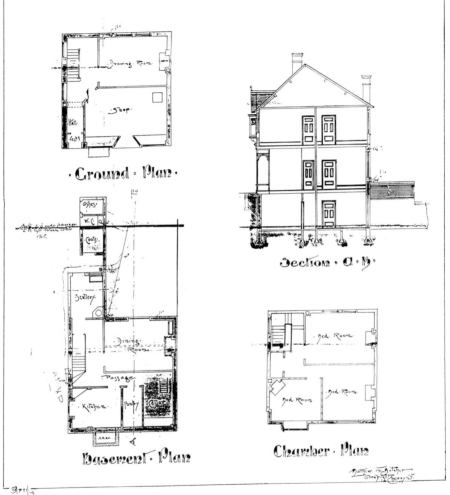

Proposed · Retail · Shop · and · Residence ·
Parade · Sutton · Coldfield · For · W. T. Jones · Esq.

· Ground · Plan ·

Section · A · B ·

Basement · Plan

Chamber · Plan

Building plans of no. 90, July 1898, by Matthew Butcher of Cherry Street.
The Parade was developed piecemeal in lots of one or two shops with different
architects — Matthew Butcher was responsible for several of them. By the time
no 102 was built, c.1905, conditions seemed to favour bigger developments, 102
being one of a block of six. Attached to the plan of no. 90 is an amendment to the
'Chamber plan' showing an enlarged room on the left containing bath, basin,
and W.C., an indication of the higher standard of housing now expected.

SUTTON COLDFIELD, ERDINGTON,

The Tripe House,

ESTABLISHED 1876.

TRIPE AND COW HEELS READY EACH EVENING AT 6 P.M.

Specialities.

Hollingsworth's Sausages

Home=made Pork Pies

ALSO

General Confectionery.

Louis Bayliss,

8, PARADE,
SUTTON COLDFIELD.

Early Advertisements, Louis Bayliss's one of the first with a 'Parade' address.

26, PARADE, SUTTON COLDFIELD.

THOMAS COLES,

Saddler, Harness and Collar Maker.

Horse Clothing, Whips, Sponges, Chamois, Brushes, &c.
Harness and other Blackings.   Stable Requisites kept in stock.

Portmanteaus and Bags repaired.   All Harness made on the premises.

Index

Tree Planting.

An Avenue of Lime Trees will be planted leading from the Town Gate towards Blackroot. This will take place at 2-30 in the afternoon of Friday the 23rd June.

The Trees will be planted in the order set out below:—

No. 1	Mr. Councillor Cartwright (Mayor)	No. 14	Mrs. Norris
2	Mrs. Cartwright (Mayoress)	15	Mrs. Parkes
		16	Mrs. Cooper
3	Mrs. Glover	17	Mrs. Clarke
4	Mrs. Walters	18	Mrs. Green
5	Mrs. Emery	19	Mrs. Willmott
6	Mrs. Seal	20	Mrs. Hooper
7	Mrs. Vale	21	Mrs. Pearson
8	Mrs. Sadler	22	Mrs. Taylor
9	Mrs. Bailey	23	Mrs. Wareing
10	Mrs. Walker	24	Mrs. Rathbone
11	Mrs. Millward	25	Mrs. Parsons
12	Miss Rabnett	26	Mrs. Reay-Nadin
13	Mrs. Appleby	27	Mrs. Clarry
		28	Mrs. T. Ellison

The Mayoress will present to each Lady a Silver Spade as a Souvenir (suitably inscribed).

A page from a King George V Coronation Souvenir, the Tree Planting is referred to on p.51.

Westwood Press Publications

THE BOOK OF BRUM .... by Ray Tennant

A SECOND BOOK OF BRUM Aware Din Urea ... by Ray Tennant

YESTERDAY'S BIRMINGHAM — Last Tram Down
the Village and Other Memories .... by Ray Tennant

THE ROYAL TOWN of SUTTON COLDFIELD
A Commemorative History .... by Douglas V. Jones

The modern sequel to The History of Sutton
SUTTON COLDFIELD 1974-1984 The Story of
a Decade .... by Douglas V. Jones

MEMORIES OF A TWENTIES CHILD .... by Douglas V. Jones

An enthralling sequel to "Memories of a 'Twenties Child"
DURATION MAN 1939-46 My War .... by Douglas V. Jones

ROUND ABOUT THE ROTUNDA Four Decades of Life
in and around Birmingham 1945-1987 ...... by Douglas V. Jones

SUTTON PARK Its History and Wildlife ...... by Douglas V. Jones

The STORY of ERDINGTON .... by Douglas V. Jones

STEAMING UP TO SUTTON How the Birmingham to Sutton
Coldfield Railway Line was built in 1862 . written by Roger Lea

SOLID CITIZENS Statues in Birmingham .... by Bridget Pugh
with drawings by Anne Irby Crews

EDGBASTON As it was .... by Douglas V. Jones

A FEAST OF MEMORIES Black Country Food and Life
at the turn of the Century .... by Marjorie Cashmore

UP THE TERRACE Down Aston and Lozells . by Ronald E. Moore

WALMLEY and Its Surroundings .... by Douglas V. Jones

FOLKLORE SUPERSTITIONS and LEGENDS of
Birmingham and The West Midlands ...... by Richard S. Brown

A HISTORY of BOLDMERE .... by Ken Williams

Obtainable from Bookshops or direct from:

Illustrated Book List available on request.

★ Please include Postage
when ordering by post.

Four or more books sent postfree.

Westwood Press
Publications

44 BOLDMERE ROAD
SUTTON COLDFIELD
0121-354 5913